P9-CRS-063

A North Carolina Naturalist—H. H. BRIMLEY

A North Carolina Naturalist

H. H. BRIMLEY

Selections From His Writings

EDITED BY

EUGENE P. ODUM

Essay Index Reprint Series

BOOKS FOR LIBRARIES PRESS
FREEPORT, NEW YORK

INTERNATIONAL STANDARD BOOK NUMBER:
0-8369-2145-3

LIBRARY OF CONGRESS CATALOG CARD NUMBER:
78-134058

PRINTED IN THE UNITED STATES OF AMERICA

PREFACE

THE LIFE OF H. H. Brimley, known affectionately by many friends as "Herb" or "Brim," spanned a very significant period in North Carolina history. Arriving in North Carolina as a young man in 1880 when the state was poor and backward, scarcely recovered from the War Between the States, he lived to see his adopted state become prosperous and progressive—a recognized leader in the South and the nation. Conversely, he witnessed the serious decline in some of Carolina's natural resources, especially the seemingly limitless supply of game and fish of which he was so fond. H. H. Brimley was not a passive onlooker during these changes, but had an active hand in making North Carolina a better place in which to live and in stemming the tide of unnecessary exploitation of its birds, mammals, and fish. While perhaps best known for his lifelong work in building up the North Carolina State Museum into a major force in the state's educational system, Brimley was a man of extraordinarily wide interests and talents. Unlike many of the naturalists and museum men of his day he did not withdraw himself completely from his fellow men and devote all his time to his specimens, but, on the contrary, he was a man's man, equally at home with and respected by hunters, fishermen, scientists, business men, and civic leaders. Because his talent for scientific work and preparation was combined with a good sense of humor and the ability to interest people, his writings are authoritative and accurate in factual material, yet singularly free from the "stuffy" style of the

v

technical paper. In his later years, especially, he became one of those rare men of science who could present facts and observations in an interesting manner without resorting to sensationalism or an overdose of sentimentalism.

I well remember my first visit with H. H. Brimley when I was a young high-school student. He took me under his wing and made me feel at home immediately. The enthusiasm and sincerity with which he worked and talked impressed me especially. In fact, H. H. Brimley and his brother C. S. did more than anyone else to encourage me to develop my interest in birds which later led me to go into teaching and research in biology as a career. Therefore, it has been my special pleasure and honor to select and edit the papers and essays brought together in this book. Some of these have been published previously; these have been reprinted largely as originally published. Other essays represent unpublished manuscripts; these have been edited only to the extent that Mr. Brimley himself might prepare them for publication. His writings, when viewed as a whole, fall into a number of distinct categories, and they have been so arranged in this volume. It should be borne in mind that Brimley's articles were written for several different levels, ranging from technical papers published in scientific journals to manuscripts prepared for newspaper and radio talks. I have tried to select and bring together under one cover representative samples of his versatile writings which are so widely scattered that otherwise they would be largely "lost." While I did not have a strictly biographical or historical objective in mind in arranging, editing, and presenting background comments for the selections, they do have some continuity even though each title is complete in itself. The chronology of the material, in a subtle sort of way, traces both the development of Mr. Brimley's personal interests and viewpoints as well as the changes in North Carolina natural history and the changing attitudes that North Carolinians have taken during his lifetime toward their rich heritage of wildlife. My only regret is that H. H. Brimley did not find time during his busy life to make this compilation. He would have done a much better job.

UNIVERSITY OF GEORGIA   *Eugene P. Odum*
January, 1949

CONTENTS

PART III

The Conservation Movement in North Carolina and Its Region

PART IV

The Giants of Nature

PART V

The Lesser Forms of Life

PART VI

The North Carolina State Museum

ILLUSTRATIONS

ix

INTRODUCTION

HERBERT HUTCHINSON BRIMLEY was born on a farm in the village of Willington near Bedford, England, on March 7, 1861. His family had been farmers for several generations raising wheat, barley, garden peas, and cattle in the valley of the Ouse River. His formal schooling was limited, but his nature education was extensive as he early showed a liking for sports and the out-of-doors in general. He later wrote that the "proximity of water enabled me to learn to swim, row a boat and paddle a canoe, handle a shotgun and fishing rod at an early age." Because prices for farm products had reached an all time low in England, partly due to competition with the New World, and having heard of opportunities in North Carolina as the result of a chance meeting with an immigration agent, all but one of the Brimley family moved to Raleigh, North Carolina, in 1880. At that time the immigrant family included besides H. H., two brothers, two sisters, and their parents. The Raleigh that they found then was not the modern city of today as is indicated by H. H. Brimley's own description written years later:

"My first impression of Raleigh was that it was without question the damndest place I had ever seen. Expecting to jump directly into the justly celebrated Sunny South, irrespective of the time of year—December 31—I found a town with unpaved streets, ruts hub-deep, frozen solid and covered with snow, and the temperature down mighty close to zero. There were some board sidewalks, but military tanks or caterpillar tractors would have been the only suitable vehicles for negotiating those streets under the prevailing conditions. The hotel, now the Old Agricultural Building, was not equipped with running water and that in the pitcher in the bedroom I occupied was frozen solid. We had to pull up the carpets and use them for blankets to keep from freezing to death the first night, no artificial heat being provided in the rooms. However, there was a bar-room in the basement, and it was there that I took my first drink of rye liquor; I did not like it as well as the Scotch and Irish on which I had been so carefully brought up. Bedford, even at that time widely known as an educational center, had paved streets and running water in the houses. Raleigh depended on wells under the sidewalks equipped with wooden pumps for its public water supply. Backyard or frontyard wells and pumps supplied some of the more pretentious residences, these private wells being sometimes situated in proximity to the so-called toilet facilities. In short, Bedford was a more or less finished town, for its time. Raleigh conveyed the impression of being comparatively raw, the cows and hogs roaming the streets giving it something of a rural atmosphere. However, there was a restless, pushing air about the place and its people that impressed me."

As might be imagined, it was not easy for the Brimleys to become established in the new town. H. H. tried unsuccessfully to farm for a year and then taught in a one-room school, also without success. Finally he teamed up with his brother, C. S., to establish a taxidermy business, which, under the name of "Brimley Brothers, Collectors and Preparers" was a going concern for about twenty years, although by no means their sole occupation during all this period. Their customers were schools and other educational institutions needing class material and private collectors who bought, sold, and swapped natural history specimens like stamps, a practice popular at that time as a hobby. While this sort of business was not the kind of occupation the Brimleys would be content to follow for a lifetime, it did enable them to become thoroughly acquainted with North Carolina animals, then almost unknown to science, and to establish for themselves a national and international reputation as the leading naturalists of the time in the South. Compared with the honeyed phrases and exaggerated claims so common in modern advertising, the following excerpt from one of the Brimleys' early catalogues is unpolished and straightforward to say the least!

To our Customers, present and future: We beg to hand you herewith our annual Price List of Zoological Material. This list annually undergoes a complete revision. Additions are made to accommodate new material acquired, eliminations to prevent advertising what we have neither got nor expect to get, and prices changed as values vary. The current issue is published on the 15th of each September, and educators and collectors ordering from such issue are abreast of the times in regard to all that the list contains. Old customers and all enquirers not receiving the new List promptly will confer a favor by notifying us of the omission. Terms: Our terms are net cash, with payment of funds at par in New York or Raleigh. As this list goes to many Zoologists with whom we are unacquainted, first orders from such should be accompanied by cash or satisfactory references. We do not ship C. O. D. to strangers.

Having established a reputation as a taxidermist, Brimley was commissioned by the Department of Agriculture in 1884 to mount waterfowl and fishes for the State Centennial Exposition at Raleigh. These specimens later became part of the collection of the State Museum. Since there was no official place on the state payroll for a taxidermist or naturalist in those days, he was listed as a "Fertilizer Inspector." In 1894 he was again hired by the Department of Agriculture as "Inspector," one of his jobs being the preparation of a fifty-foot Wright Whale from a huge pile of bones lying on the Museum floor. The finished job today greets the visitor as he enters the Museum and has served to impress upon thousands of visitors the largeness of nature. The very next year, 1895, Brimley was appointed Curator of the Museum, a position which he held until 1928, when the title was changed to Director. He served as Director until his retirement in 1937.

During this period the museum grew in size from 2,000 to over 20,000 feet of floor space devoted to exhibits which attracted over 200,000 visitors yearly just prior to the Second World War.

During the twenty years following his 1884 work for the State Exposition, Brimley organized or had a prominent part in North Carolina exhibits in various exhibitions over the country, for example, the Chicago World's Fair of 1893, the St. Louis Exhibition of 1904, the Boston Food Fair of 1906, and the Jamestown Exposition of 1907. These exhibits brought not only personal recognition to H. H. but also valuable advertising to the state when most needed. He was a member of the International Jury of Awards during the St. Louis and Jamestown fairs and was appointed Executive Commissioner to the Panama Pacific Exhibition scheduled for San Francisco, but cancelled owing to the outbreak of the First World War.

Very shortly after becoming Curator of the Museum, Brimley began what was to develop into a lifelong and intimate friendship with another North Carolinian, T. Gilbert Pearson, who was destined to become one of the leading crusaders for bird protection in our times. An ardent hunter and fisherman himself, Brimley was quick to recognize the seriousness of the unrestricted slaughter of all forms of native life. He was one of Pearson's staunchest supporters at a time when conservation was not popular and the going rough. H. H. joined with Pearson and C. S. Brimley in co-authoring the *Birds of North Carolina* which was one of the first state bird books in the South and long remained a classic. This book, which was widely distributed throughout the state, did much to stimulate interest in and appreciation of native birds. One of the last major contributions of all three of the authors was the revision and republication of this book in 1942, thus providing a second generation of North Carolinians with a fine reference work. Brimley also collaborated with Hugh M. Smith in preparing, in 1907, *Fishes of North Carolina,* a book which today is still considered the best state work on fish in the southeast.

It was on one of his eastern North Carolina field trips that Herbert Brimley met Bessie Love at White Lake. They were married in Wilmington on February 28, 1913. His wife was a constant companion on many trips to the eastern Carolina wildlands which they both loved.

H. H. Brimley was a very active participant in scientific and semi-scientific organizations. He was a founder of the North Carolina Academy of Science, Raleigh Natural History Club, Raleigh Bird Club, and North Carolina Bird Club, serving as president of the latter. He held lifelong memberships in the American Association of Museums, the American Society of Mammalogists, the American Museum of Natural History, and the American Ornithologists' Union. In 1934 he was elected a full Member of the latter organization, a class of membership restricted to 150 of the leading ornithologists of the country.

Throughout his long life H. H. Brimley was an ardent hunter and fisherman and was a frequent contributor to sporting magazines. He always looked forward with much anticipation to an annual deer and waterfowl hunting expedition to eastern Carolina. He thoroughly enjoyed the long hours at a deer stand. If no deer came, as might frequently be the case, he obtained pleasure from observing the lesser life about him, as, for example, the Phoebe which insisted on lighting on his gun barrel and picking off mosquitoes from his clothing (see his account in Part V). Above all, Brimley was a true sportsman of the highest type, one that all those who obtain pleasure from the pursuit of game and fish would do well to emulate.

Although his first impressions of Raleigh may have been a bit disconcerting, Brimley became one of the city's greatest boosters. He was very active in civic affairs, especially in later years when the struggle for earning a living was not so great. He served as president of the Rotary Club of the city and was one of the very few of its members to be elected to honorary lifetime membership. He was also active in Scout work and served as president of the local council of the Boy Scouts of America.

The writing of poetry was another of Brimley's hobbies and another illustration of the great versatility of his interests and talents. His verses appeared frequently in North Carolina newspapers and three of them were selected for inclusion in the book,

North Carolina Poems, edited by E. C. Brooks and published by North Carolina Education, Raleigh, 1912. As with his prose, his poems were never overly sentimental but were vigorous and permeated with subtle humor. Several of his poems are included in this volume.

Perhaps because he felt that his technical training in biology was deficient, Mr. Brimley placed a very high value on books which became to him both a source of education and inspiration. During his lifetime he built up a fine library of natural history works at the Museum. In June, 1941, this Museum library was officially designated by the Board of Agriculture of North Carolina as the Brimley Library of Natural History "as a tribute to his lengthy and efficient service." After his death his personal library was presented by Mrs. H. H. Brimley to the State College of Agriculture of the University of North Carolina in Raleigh where it is designated as the H. H. Brimley Memorial Library of Natural History.

Although retiring from administrative duties as Director of the State Museum in 1937, Brimley did not "retire" in the literal sense of the word, but remained actively at work as Curator of Zoology for another ten years. Some of the manuscripts written during this period are among his best. At the time of his death on April 4, 1946, at the age of eighty-five, he was the oldest active North Carolina state employee, and one of its most respected and beloved.—Eugene P. Odum

PART ONE

Early Interests and Explorations

EDITOR'S NOTE

As was indicated in the preceding biographical sketch, H. H. Brimley and his brother, C. S., turned to natural-history collecting as a means of establishing themselves in the New World. During this early period, the brothers contributed numerous short, largely descriptive articles to natural-history journals, especially the old Ornithologist and Oologist, *which ceased publication in 1893. Several examples of these early papers from H. H.'s pen are reprinted in this section together with four short selections written years later as Brimley looked back on the "Gay Nineties" period.*

The reader should remember that before 1900 there were virtually no laws restricting the taking or sale of game, or non-game animals, for that matter. Brimley's description of the professional market hunters of eastern Carolina in the selection "Old Days on Currituck" illustrates the then prevailing attitude towards waterfowl, when anything edible was shot to the limit and sold on the market for a few paltry cents. The average person thought nothing of this unrestricted slaughter because the game seemed so abundant then, an attitude not uncommon today concerning things (not waterfowl) of which we still have a good supply.

Likewise, the nature lover of today should not think too harshly of Mr. Brimley for his egg collecting activities, since this was accepted procedure for the naturalist of that time even though bird students of today have largely turned to other methods of study. Also, it should be emphasized that egg collecting, unlike the slaughter of ducks concentrated on restricted wintering grounds, was rarely damaging to the species, since most species build again very quickly when their nests are destroyed.

2

With Rope and Irons [*]

Plenty of information as to the finding of nests of certain birds can be gleaned from the *Ornithologist and Oologist,* but the writers usually leave one in blissful ignorance of the way by which they take a difficult nest. Perhaps this omission is a delicate compliment to the inventive power of the average collector. Most collectors can take a rare nest in some way or another and I would be glad to read some descriptions of the methods used.

Two years ago climbing irons were an unknown quantity to me and a rope just sufficiently thin to give a bad hand-hold was the only means in use in going up a tree. A Red-shouldered Hawk's nest thirty feet above the grit in a big white oak is an example. A stone attached to a light line was thrown over the lowest limb (about twenty feet up) and by means of this line, the rope was drawn over the limb and made fast. The tree was too large to hug and the rope cut my hands pretty badly, but three eggs was

[*] *Ornithologist and Oologist,* XIII (October, 1888), 150-51.

the result. The second laying of the same birds was fifty feet up in a pine, twenty-five feet to the lowest limb. The same method was employed, but the tree being huggable the work was not so hard, though quite hard enough for two rather dull eggs.

The next March on passing the nest, two projections appeared on the edge of the structure suggesting "Bubo." Thrashing the tree with a long pole didn't have any effect and I about gave it up, but tried a load of sixes to satisfy myself. At the crack of the gun a pair of mighty wings beat the air for a second and Mrs. Owl came crashing down. The rope was fetched and put in place and one well-incubated egg brought safely down.

A Great Crested Flycatcher was watched into a knot-hole in the bare trunk of a fair sized elm, several feet below the lowest limb. The usual method put the rope over the limb, a short stick was tied to the middle of the rope and then drawn up till it hung a foot or two below the hole, the end of the rope being then made fast to a sapling nearby. As the hole was too small to admit my hand, my brother improvised an egg scoop made out of a small forked twig, with a piece of his coat lining pinned in place. I went up the rope to the cross stick which afforded a good seat and scooped out five eggs.

The rope business got to be rather tiring, so climbers were procured, and are now considered as much of a necessity as a gun. When they came to hand, nothing would do but to try them at once. I strapped them on, waddled out to the largest tree in the yard, a small elm. I took a firm grip of the tree with my hands, shut my eyes, dug in the spurs and walked right up to the first limb. Then looking down from the dizzy height I found my feet to be at least three feet from the ground. This gave me confidence and when I did get to a sure enough tree, I rose to the occasion.

Pine Warblers' nests were found from the end of March. Early in April full sets began to be in order and with the help of the climbers I did not find much difficulty in reaching the level of the nests, few of which, however, could be reached by hand from the tree trunk. A long, slender pointed stick was used for taking those not within reach. The pointed end of the pole was carefully thrust through both sides of the nest about half way of its height and the nest being a well-woven structure the nest was in every case broken loose from its hold without material injury. This loosening process has to be done very carefully, however, otherwise the spring of the pole is liable to break the nest away suddenly and jerk out the contents. Out of ten nests taken but one shared that fate. Sixty feet up in a pine swaying in a strong breeze, the nest was at least twelve feet away. The pole was more springy than usual, the wind seemed to freshen and I seemed getting scared. In my hurry to get the eggs and come down I pulled the nest away with a jerk, it turned completely over and an empty nest was my only reward for an old-fashioned climb. It was all the more annoying from the fact that I believe from one or two scraps of egg shells I picked up below the nest that this set was of the rarest type with red spots on a pure white ground.

I have found a common reed fishing pole about the best stick to use in this method of taking nests. I carry a hundred feet of light line, the pole and egg box at end, coil the line on a clear ground below the tree, tie the other end to my belt and go aloft. When the nest is taken and packed in the egg box, the line lowers it to the ground, and a knot tied when the box has reached terra firma gives the height of nest.

A Brown-headed Nuthatch had a nest fifteen feet up a very rotten twenty-foot stub on the edge of three feet of water. A loop in the middle of the rope was passed around the stub and drawn taut after having been pushed up nearly to the hole. My brother on the land side holding one end of the rope, lowered the stub into the water as I pulled it down with the other end of the rope, after wading across. The stick broke into several pieces as it struck the water, but we floated from it five handsome eggs all too far incubated to be saved.

Another Nuthatch was occupying a hole twelve or fifteen feet up a stub, too rotten to bear my weight, and too solid and heavy to pull over. Six feet from it grew a slender birch sapling, leaning away from the stub and likewise too weak to bear me. I dragged up a couple of ten-foot fence rails and tied them together with my belt and game bag strap, close to one end after being crossed, just leaving enough fork to hold the birch sapling when the long ends were stuck in the mud on the side away from the stub and far enough apart to give a wide base. This gave a very shaky climb and foothold as my weight caused the ends of the rails to sink in the mud, but after a good deal of hard work tearing out and cutting away the half rotten wood surrounding the nest, at full arms-length I managed to secure what there was, an incomplete set of three.

A Barred Owl was rapped out of the top of a twenty-foot birch stub, standing in the water. The outer wood was rotten and I had to tear away the shell with my fingers as I went up to expose a hard enough surface for the spurs to bite. The two eggs were put in my hat with some cotton and the hat replaced on my head. I did not pack in the egg box as I had all my work cut out in climbing to the old rotten stub and could only use one hand at once. The eggs which came down safely were addled —putrid, I should say and I don't think I could have blown them without parting with my dinner; I got a whiff of them at long range as my brother was calmly removing the contents and I left the room. If they had only broken when in my hat!

Foot-Rule and Scales[*]

T HERE IS NOTHING better calculated to knock the romance out
of the enormous specimens of fish, flesh and fowl that become
the prey of the hunter and fisherman than these two small instru-
ments—foot-rule and scales.

Several "large" eagles have been mentioned in the *Ornithologist and Oologist* at different times and quite a little discussion
arose on the question of size. I well remember the first eagle I
ever handled. He was alive, one wing being broken, and by the
time I had got him safely laid out I began to speculate on his
spread of wing. The specimen was an adult "bald" and I could
not feel satisfied under seven and a half or eight feet across the
wings—something to talk about. The foot-rule was introduced
and gave the returns as six feet six inches.

A much larger adult specimen of the same species was handled
shortly after but circumstances were such that I had no oppor-

* *Ornithologist and Oologist*, XV, No. 9 (September, 1890), 139-40.

tunity of measuring. A conservative estimate would have given this one some eight or eight and a half feet spread. It was probably not over seven. I got hold of another one that seemed very large, this time an immature "bald," second year I think. I fully expected seven and a half feet this time; foot-rule said six feet nine inches.

I was down the creek after Louisiana Water-thrush nests last spring and came on a chicken snake lying stretched out on the bare ground. "Seven feet, or I'm a liar," I remarked to myself confidently as my eye measured every inch of his length. I fully believe that anyone used to measuring snakes only by eye would have estimated that one at seven and a half or eight feet. It was an enormous specimen for this region. Its correct length by the foot-rule was five feet nine inches.

I remember being told some years ago by a man who had twice doubled Cape Horn in a sailing ship, that the Albatrosses killed in the Pacific and brought aboard ship measured twenty-eight or thirty feet from tip to tip. Science comes along with a foot-rule and says they don't grow that large now-a-days. Condors are or were popularly supposed to measure twelve or fifteen feet across the wings, but collectors of these large specimens usually left their foot-rule at home.

I had a mean trick played on me the other day. I was one of a small fishing party, and on reaching the river and commencing operations one of the crowd produced a carpenter's rule, and remarked that he was now ready to record the size of all large fish caught, having brought his instrument along in the interests of truth. Among other things we caught a gar that was at least three feet long and would have been recorded as such had not that miserable carpenter's rule said it was twenty-four inches only.

Winter before last I caught my first otter. I was as proud as a dog with two tails, and sat on a log and admired my game, good fashion, before making any estimates. I knew very well that the book size of an otter was four feet and a half long, weight, twenty-five pounds. Mine I estimated at four feet by twenty pounds, but before I got home I thought he weighed forty. Foot-rule said three feet six inches, and scales said fifteen pounds. I have trapped a number of others since then and can now estimate the size of an otter pretty well.

Early last spring I was crossing a ridge of woods and came on a possum sitting in the fork of a black jack some twenty-five feet up. Needing his skin and not wishing to make a sieve of it I manoeuvred around until his body was protected by the fork, leaving only his head visible. After shooting at him four times with tens, sixes and B. B.'s, climbing for him, knocking him out, catching him on the ground and killing him, I discovered what I thought before, that I had secured a large possum, though poor. On my way home I met two men going fishing who exclaimed at the large size of my game. I handed it to one of them asking what he thought it weighed. He "hefted" it and remarked that "that possum'll dress eight pounds." I expressed surprise as my estimate of its weight was about seven pounds, gross. He handed it to the other man who likewise gave its weight at eight pounds when dressed. I met another old fellow a little further on, a man who knows what's what in possum lore. He also considered it a big one but gave no specified weight. People here who don't use scales consider a possum should weigh six or eight or more pounds when dressed to be a large one, and you can *hear* of them up to ten or twelve pounds. On putting mine on the scales he weighed exactly five and a half pounds, gross, equivalent I suppose to three and a half or four pounds, net. My faith in ten pounders is small since then.

With regard to the use of foot-rule and scales by fishermen I can only say "don't." Give us liberty (to estimate the size of our fish) or give us death.

Some Random Notes on
Egg Collecting*

FOLLOWING OUR ARRIVAL in Raleigh in 1880, the main activity of my brother, C. S., and I in endeavoring to keep the justly celebrated wolf from the not-too-securely-fastened door was a crude grade of custom taxidermy together with the collecting of bird skins and eggs for wealthy men in the big cities, who vied with each other over the comparative magnitude of their collections.

It was soon discovered that eggs, to be acceptable to the large collectors had to be cleanly and carefully blown through one small circular hole drilled in the side of the egg, and that definite data must be provided for the "set," no single eggs or incomplete sets being accepted. The data required absolute identification, date of taking, type of nest, height above ground, situation, and approximate degree of incubation.

A rather bulky outfit was carried on our collecting trips. This included a pair of climbing irons, with extra long spurs, kept

* The Chat, VI, No. 3 (May, 1942), 37-40.

very sharp, about a hundred feet of hand-woven string (seine cord), some seventy-five feet of light, strong rope, several empty cigar boxes, plenty of cotton batting, notebook, grappling hooks for taking nests beyond the reach of one's hands, and some kind of measuring device. All being carried in a capacious game bag, and irons slung under one arm by a shoulder strap.

The spurs on those tree-climbing irons are longer and have a more slender taper than those used by telephone linemen, who only have to climb bare poles. In climbing trees the bark has to be penetrated before a safe hold can be secured in the wood underneath, which calls for a much heavier stroke with the spur at each upward step.

I remember the time when I started up a big white oak after a hawk's nest. It was an unusually large tree, with enormous limbs springing from a rather short trunk. I could not get my arms much more than half way around it, and had to depend on finger-tip holds in the crevices of the bark. I dug my spurs in as deep as I could, but one stroke failed to reach the wood when I was about five feet above the ground, the bark in which it was imbedded slipped as soon as my weight came on it, and I promptly hit terra firma. I don't believe the old nest had anything in it, anyway.

Searching for the nests of the Louisiana Water-thrush was always an interesting experience, as their nesting sites with us were strictly confined to certain very definite localities and locations. First, one had to find a small, free-flowing stream, the upper waters of which ran through fairly open woods, with steep banks rising not less than three feet above the water-level. Starting in at the lowest part of the stream that had suitable banks, we would wade up the branch with eyes peeled for any possible nest site, which was usually on the ground back of a tussock, or cluster of ferns, and remarkably well hidden. Even a careful scrutiny might easily miss a nest under such conditions, unless occupied at the time, when the sudden flight of its occupant would be a give-away. Only occasionally did we ever find more than one pair of birds occupying an individual stream.

The following is a verbatim copy of my field notes on the taking of a nest of this species: "April 30, 1889. 1/5 La. Water-thrush, in hollow of perpendicular bank 3 feet above running water. Nest well overhung and entrance almost hidden by hanging rootlets: of wet dead leaves, grass stems and rootlets and lined with finer ditto."

Nests of birds in general were frequently discovered by listening to and following singing males around the approximate start of their nesting, and sometimes by scattering scraps of lint cotton in the general location where one might expect to find certain species that were not averse to making use of cotton in their nest-building activities.

The following detailed description of the taking a set of eggs will illustrate the methods used in securing nests built in fairly tall trees, where the use of the irons was imperative.

A pair of Pine Warblers had been discovered building in a tall, slender Loblolly (Old Field) Pine in a grove of similar trees directly back of where the Louis Smith Dairy operates on the old Poole Road. When sufficient time had elapsed to assure the completion of the nest and the laying of the eggs, the trip was made to secure them.

At the foot of the tree I strapped on the climbers and started up. I didn't much like the job as the tree was very slender and swaying quite a lot in the strong wind that was blowing—to say nothing of the fact that the nest was a long, long way from the ground. After climbing about halfway to the nest, I stopped to look over the situation. The conclusion was that when my weight reached the very small trunk near which the nest was situated any extra puff of wind might easily swing the tree-top, with my weight added, to the point where a dangerous situation might develop. So I climbed a little higher, got out the rope (to which reference has been previously made), tied it fast to the tree and tossed the rest of it to the ground. On reaching ground-level, the lower part of the rope was carried directly to windward, drawn tight and made fast to the base of another pine that happened to be in the right place.

I soon found, on reclimbing the tree, that the guy rope was doing its full duty so I continued until level with the nest, which was quickly secured. The four eggs were wrapped separately in strips of cotton and then restored to the nest, which was then packed securely in one of the cigar boxes and carefully lowered to the ground by means of the seine cord. As soon as the box touched the ground a knot was made in the cord before dropping it. On reaching the ground, unfastening the rope and dropping it as I reached the place of attachment, the measuring unit was brought into use and the line between the knot and the box measured, which gave the height of the nest from the ground, in this instance, 70 feet.

Previous to the adoption of packing the eggs and then lowering them by means of a cord, they had at times been carried down either in one's hat or in the mouth, neither method being particularly recommended as either safe or very enjoyable, under certain readily understood conditions; such things as addled eggs being known to occur in even the best regulated bird families!

COLLECTING IN ENGLAND

Prior to even those remote days, my brother and I had collected eggs during our youthful days in England. We had access to several books on British Birds and their eggs, one with colored drawings of the eggs of many of the species. Of course, we usually took only one egg from a nest, blowing it by word of mouth from a big hole in the larger end, and the air being forced through a slightly smaller hole at the other end, neither egg-drill nor blowpipe being then known, at least to us.

Fortunately for us, we were able to capitalize our ornithological knowledge by participating in the bounties provided for the taking of English Sparrows (European House Sparrow) and their eggs. As I now remember these transactions, we received the princely honorarium of two cents a dozen for eggs and two cents each for adults. Just think of it! Only twelve dozen eggs, and between us we had a sum of money equivalent to the U. S. quarter of a dollar jingling in our pants!

The find that gave us our greatest thrill was the discovery of a nest of the Long-tailed Titmouse, a rather rare bird with us and the builder of a most remarkable nest. It is oval in shape and completely enclosed except for a small opening in one side near the top. The outer wall is thick and composed of "shredded wool, green moss, spider silk and lichens, artfully interwoven until it completely surrounds the five-inch interior." The inside is then thickly lined with feathers. Coward in his *Birds of the British Isles,* states: "Considerably over two thousand [feathers] have been counted from one nest." The number of eggs laid by the Long-tailed Titmouse varies from 8 to 12, normally, with one record of 16 young being found in a nest. This Tit is a tiny, dainty bird, equipped with an exceptionally long tail.

A few words about the justly celebrated Starling on his native heath. Among the farm buildings was a large, brick pigeon house, rectangular in shape, with the walls 4 or 5 feet thick at the base. The walls were about 20 feet high on the inside, decreasing in thickness by the width of a brick every two or three layers of masonry, thus forming a series of steps that made climbing easy. At each step, on all four sides of the building, holes had been left in the brickwork as nesting sites for the pigeons, and many of these holes were used by usurping Starlings. Having always been impressed with the belief that the Starlings sucked the eggs of the pigeons, the eggs of the former were destroyed whenever found.

It was quite generally believed that if you slit the tongue of a Starling, it could talk. It never occurred to me that it would have to be taught to say words, after the operation, my idea being that, once the tongue was slit, its happy owner would at once start a general conversation on any matter that came to mind.

Several hundred pigeons inhabited the structure. One other farm in the village boasted a Dove House, the two being about half a mile apart, and the inhabitants of the two intermingled as they saw fit. A percentage of the young reached the table in the form of "pigeon pies" and, when the house became too crowded, the surplus of adults was sold alive for shooting matches at live pigeons, a perfectly legitimate form of outdoor recreation, approved by our best people, in those benighted days.

Old Times on Currituck [*]

THE WATERFOWL OF CURRITUCK

On the stretches of the Sound to westward,
  And over the Sound to east
The fowl are adrift in thousands
  Alert at their watery feast;
And down in the southward reaches—
  As over the bay to north—
Are many more thousands winging
  Their aerials back and forth.

The broad and long expanses
  Of shoal and feeding ground
Are alive with countless myriads
  As nowhere else are found:

[*] Reprinted from *North Carolina Wildlife Conservation*, VII, No. 3 (March, 1943), 8-13, with the addition of the poem "The Waterfowl of Currituck" which was originally printed in the *Charlotte Observer*.

Acres of fowl on the water
  And clouds of them in the air,—
There's naught among Nature's pictures
  Can ever with this compare.

Great swans in their snowy whiteness
  Are feeding along the shoals,
Their long necks dipping and rising
  Where the short, quick wavelet rolls;
While geese in their tens of thousands
  Are honking loud and clear,
With sentinels out to warn them
  If boat or man draw near.

The canvas-back and the red-head
  On the celery beds at feed,
Raft up into floating islands
  Or swift through the air lanes speed:
The mallard and black duck loiter,
  With many a strident quack,
In the ponds and slues of the marshes,
  Aloof from the beaten track.

The wood duck, teal and gadwall
  Drive in as evening falls
To the shallow ponds of the sedges,
  As each to the other calls:
The white snow geese of the beaches
  Line up like a drift of snow,
At home in the gentlest breezes
  As well as the wildest blow.

Made wise by constant shooting
  (Experience dearly bought!),
These fowl are no hand-raised pheasants,
  But graduates—strictly taught!

Left, H. H. Brimley at the age of eighteen. *Right*, Mr. Brimley at the age of forty-five. This picture was taken in September, 1906. *Below*, The Brimley brothers. Left to right, Fred, H. H., C. S. Fred remained in England when the other two sought their fortunes in North Carolina. This picture was made on the occasion of Fred's only visit to Raleigh.

Here Mr. Brimley is mounting a specimen of the Glassy Ibis, a rare bird in North Carolina. (*N. C. State Museum*)

They are wise to decoys, well painted
  To the marks of each waterfowl kind,
They are wise to the battery's inmate—
  To the man in the off-shore blind.

And over the water the eagles
  Keep a watch for the crippled fowl
While those that crawl out on the marshes
  Fall a prey to the great horned owl.
There is death in the windy reaches
  And under the marsh's lee,
But they've found them a haven of safety
  On the breast of the open sea.

My first direct knowledge of Currituck Sound was in February, 1884, just fifty-nine years ago, and many of the impressions experienced at that time were so deeply engraved on my memory that they continue to show up clearly at the present day.

Reaching Currituck was not easy in those days as that section of the State then possessed no railway facilities. By rail to Norfolk was the first lap; thence by steamer up the Elizabeth River, through the Albemarle and Chesapeake canal and North River into Currituck Sound. The canal was again entered at the south end of Coinjock Bay, my getting-off place being the settlement of Coinjock. From there, across Church Island to the Midyette place on the sound was by ox-cart.

My business there was to collect and preserve specimens of waterfowl for exhibition purposes at the State Exposition that was to be held during the whole of the following October at the old State Fair Grounds near Raleigh.

My headquarters being situated about the center of the market-hunting industry, most of the specimens secured were purchased from the professional gunners. But I did some personal collecting, as on "Bluebird" days the market hunters would not bother to go out, when I would secure the loan of a battery and pick up a few specimens that way.

The gas boat was unknown in those days, all boat movement

being by sail or man-power. The sail-boats were known as "canoes." They were large dug-outs, roomy enough to carry five or six head of cattle, or horses, and they were used by the duck-hunters in carrying their batteries to and from the shooting grounds, with the stand of decoys, occupying one or more skiffs and towed by the canoe.

These crafts were built up of three dug-out pieces dowelled together, the inside framing assisting in fastening the three units to tight, waterproof joints. They were heavy crafts but safe and seaworthy, their sail-plan being the more or less standardized sprit-sail and jib rig, perhaps the most handy and convenient rig ever used on a comparatively small sail-boat.

The skiffs were never rowed or paddled, as the shallow waters of the sound made poling a much more efficient method of propulsion.

There were ducks and geese on the sound in those days. One afternoon I tried to count roughly the number of Canada Geese in a straggling line of flocks that was crossing Church's Island for their night's resting place in Coinjock Bay. My estimate was well above the ten thousand mark, and that flight represented only a small part of the myriads frequenting the sound both north and south from my viewpoint.

My host, Uncle Ned Midyette, owned four batteries and employed the gunners to man them, two men constituting the crew of each. He also employed a boy to do odd jobs around the house whose first duty every morning was, as soon as light enough to distinguish objects, to take his gun and inspect several miles of shore-line to pick up crippled ducks that had swum ashore during the night, it being a well-known habit of ducks to come ashore when wounded.

One day, when the boy was hauling wood with the ox-cart, he asked me if I wanted an eagle or two. When I replied in the affirmative, he told me that he had just driven his cart directly beneath a pair of white-headed (Bald) eagles perched in medium-sized pines a little way back in the woods, and that they took no notice of his outfit. If I could go with him, he felt quite sure that he could take me directly under them, the rest being up to me. So I slipped a couple of heavy loads in my gun and we started for the woods, with the writer sitting on the bottom boards of the cart with his legs hanging over at the rear-end, all ready for a quick slide out when under the birds. He did his part all right, but when I slid out of the cart almost directly under the eagles, expecting to get one with each barrel, my foot slipped and I made a clean miss on both! Since then I have often wondered what sort of a tale the boy told his fellow-employees about the poor marksmanship of the city feller who couldn't hit as big an object as an eagle when it was almost sitting on his head! But I did kill an eagle before I left—while after ducks.

The following are the approximate prices the gunners were getting for their fowl, cash on the spot by the regular buyers, all prices per pair except as otherwise noted: Canvasback, $1.00; Redhead, 50 cents; "common duck," 30 cents; small ducks, as Teal, Ruddy, Bufflehead, etc., 25 cents, with four ducks constituting a pair! Canada Geese brought 50 cents each.

At that time, of course, no refrigeration facilities were available, though a small amount of icing may have been done. The usual method, however, was to allow the fowl to hang up over night to cool off, they being packed in barrels the next morning and shipped to Norfolk by steamer.

One night a very interesting visitor made a call at the house, another of the Midyettes, I think. He was quite an old man, but an interesting talker. Among other things, he mentioned the fact that he remembered the first "karasene" that was ever seen on Currituck, secured from a wreck, I think he said, but I fail to remember whether they burned whale oil or candles previous to the invasion of kerosene. On asking if he could notice any decrease in the number of fowl frequenting the sound, he said that he thought the geese were not as plentiful as in years gone by. Further questioning brought out the statement that he made his best bag of geese a number of years back, on a snowy day, when he and his two sons killed a hundred and three, using "flint and steel" guns. Considering the speaker's apparent age, one might believe that the episode referred to could have happened back in the eighteen forties, when the percussion gun was rapidly replacing the flintlock. However, I saw a flintlock in actual use a year later (in 1885) when a boy living near Cherry Point, Craven County, was seen taking such a weapon with him early one morning on a quest for ducks in Hancock's Creek. This was the only time I ever saw a gun of this type in actual use.

Batteries have been outlawed for a number of years now, and it may be a matter of interest—particularly to the younger generation—to submit a description of an old-time battery and its outfit as used on Currituck Sound in the eighteen eighties.

Another name for the device was "sink box," which is far more descriptive than the name commonly used, which means hardly anything in this connection.

The box itself was a coffin-shaped affair, of such dimensions as to afford a fairly close fit, both in length and width, for an average sized man lying on his back, its depth being such that no part of the occupant could be seen when the box was viewed from the side.

When in use, a small pillow, or cushion, raised the head until the eyes were on a level with the rims of the box. At this same level a rigid deck some three feet wide was attached on all four sides and sloping slightly down towards the water, with flexible floating wings attached to all sides of the fixed deck, and with a particularly long extension at the head end. These wings, rising and falling with the motion of the surface water, tended to keep it from running up the fixed deck and so into the box. An added precaution against this most uncomfortable possibility consisted of strips of sheet lead an inch or two wide that were tacked along their inner edges, so that they could be turned slightly by their outer edges whenever the surface became rough enough to warrant such procedure. When finished, the whole upper surface of the complete battery was painted a flat slaty-gray, which made it almost invisible a short distance away.

At its best, a battery was always a clumsy affair and awkward to handle, and setting one out and taking it up again on a cold, windy day was no job for weaklings.

It was securely anchored by the head, with a dragging anchor of lighter weight out over the tail end, the latter to prevent too much swinging sidewise.

Possibly, 150 decoys was about an average "stand" for a single battery. I have seen much larger stands used as well as many not so large. The best arrangement of the decoys is about as indicated in the plan shown, with the bulk of the decoys concentrated about at right angles to the box on the left side of the man lying therein. For a left-handed gunner, the arrangement would be reversed. The remainder of the decoys should gradually taper off in width and be more widely scattered down wind from the larger concentration near the battery.

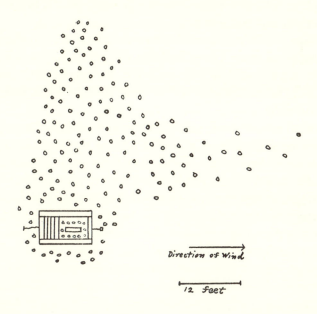

Direction of Wind

12 feet

Movable ballast was used to sink the battery to its most effective level in the water, the ballast consisting of cast iron decoys, weighing about twenty-five pounds each. The number of iron ducks used was variable, perhaps ten being an average. There are twelve shown on the deck around the box in the plan. They were painted in keeping with the wooden decoys, and each iron decoy was fastened with a stout line to one of its wooden brethren, so that if the weather should turn rough enough to threaten water in the box, some of the iron ducks could be slid overboard and thus raise the battery to a safer level.

The professional gunners, and some experienced amateurs, would take two guns with them in the box. The thirty-two inch barrels made it easier to rest the muzzles on the foot-board, which should always be done for reasons of safety. The guns usually used by the market gunners were double-barreled ten gauge weapons, with 32-inch barrels, and hammers. Automatics and repeaters came along at a later date.

I have tried this method of shooting on a number of occasions but have nearly always had better shooting from a blind, though the battery was a deadly method of taking water-fowl when practiced by experienced professionals. There is a Chesapeake Bay record of more than five hundred ducks killed in one day's shooting by a market hunter using two guns in his battery. On Currituck, bags of a hundred a day from a battery were not rare enough to get one's name in the paper.

A now-deceased friend of mine, a crack shot on ducks, substituting for a market hunter at his request, once averaged about 130 a day for three successive days, and that was well within the present century.

I never saw or heard anything to make me believe that "punt" guns had ever been in general use on Currituck Sound, at least in comparatively recent years, as they had been in some parts of Chesapeake Bay. But, some years later, the State Museum was given the choice of purchasing one or both of two guns of this type, from a resident of Currituck County. We secured the better of the two, which is now on display in the Museum. Our specimen is a flintlock, weighing nearly one hundred pounds. The barrel is eight feet long, with a bore of one and a half inches. The standard load for this weapon would have been about one pound of shot driven by an ounce and a half to two ounces of black powder. Larger swivel guns, breech-loaders, were used in later years, some of them being handsomely finished pieces to be used with nitro powders. So far as I can learn, no gun of this more modern type ever found its way to Currituck.

I have often heard of crow roosts, but never saw one, though I am confident that a very heavily-populated roost of this character was in existence at the time of my first visit, situated on the Banks in a northeasterly direction from Church's Island. Every afternoon when I happened to be out of doors, vast numbers of crows were seen crossing the sound in the direction indicated. From about an hour before sunset until dusk the flight was fairly steady though, of course, by no means regular. There must have been many thousands of crows congregating for the night somewhere in the region indicated, but it was a long way off and, with the transportation facilities what they were, no attempt was made to ascertain the facts.

It goes almost without saying that a majority of the inhabitants of the shores of the sound made most of their winter's income directly or indirectly from the commercial hunting of wildfowl. During the summer months many of the market hunters shifted to fishing, Black Bass and White Perch being their main objectives. About that time, or a few years later, the commercial catch of Black Bass alone, from that region, reached a total of about half a million pounds annually, which is quite a lot of bass!

On one of those "Bluebird" days, the weather felt so much like a day in late spring that I experimented with a swim in the sound. But you can bet your last dollar that I didn't stay in the water very long!

There were—and are—no Brant on Currituck, this small species of goose being strictly a salt-water bird with us. But Snow Geese and Whistling Swan were plentiful, though in somewhat restricted areas, these geese feeding almost exclusively on the east side of the sound, and mainly on land, as they now do on Pea Island.

It should also be remembered that in those remote days Lake Mattamuskeet was used but little by wildfowl, due to the absence of suitable food therein. It was in no sense a competitor with Currituck Sound then, Mattamuskeet having only come into its own as a great congregating spot for swan, geese and ducks since it has been partly drained and the waterlevel kept low.

I had my first taste of young swan, baked, on that trip and, later, had a young swan sent me on several occasions for use on the home table. I need not caution my readers not to strain their teeth on an *old* swan, as such a feat has long been contrary to the law—and never has been highly recommended!

Cape Hatteras in Storm and Shine*

THERE ARE FEW names more widely known in the United States or localities about which a greater ignorance prevails than Cape Hatteras. Situated as it is at the angle where the long strip of sand beach from Cape Henry south turns at a right angle to the westward, with the widest part of Pamlico Sound between it and the mainland and with the beach, both west and north, cut into several islands by inlets from sound to ocean, its position is most isolated. No means of transportation exist along the beach and, with the nearest railway station from which a regular transportation route is operated nearly a hundred miles away, it is an easier place to talk about than to visit. Moreover, what travel facilities there are are not of the floating palace kind. A small river steamer runs from Elizabeth City to Roanoke Island and from the latter place to the Cape a still smaller "gasoliner" is the "only way." And sometimes, in very rough weather, there isn't any "only way."

* Written for the *Charlotte Daily Observer* in 1905.

Some day it will be a great resort—but not in my day I hope. Its very remoteness constitutes no small part of its present charm. Its marshes and beaches; its woods and ponds; its sound and ocean; the smooth, flat, harmless looking sandy point of the dreaded Cape itself, all go to make it a place of absorbing interest. And seaward, south-easterly from the point, unseen and un-indicated in calm weather, below the surface of the restless tides run the Diamond Shoals, stabbing the Atlantic with a tongue of fear for nine miles or more from the point of the Cape. Seven miles beyond the outer edge of the shoals rides the Diamond Shoal Light Vessel, its heavy mushroom anchors gripping the sands in thirty six fathoms of water, a fairway for ships of any tonnage. And, with this vessel's warning lights well beyond the danger point and the great tower of the Hatteras as Lighthouse—the highest lighthouse tower in the United States, by the way—near the base of the shoals on shore, wrecks here are not as numerous as formerly though still numerous enough. And the life savers are there too; with one station at the Cape proper, another at Creeds Hill and still another at Durants, all well equipped with modern outfits, and within reach of wrecks on the Diamond.

The general run of the work of the life savers is not of the spectacular kind that sometimes gets into the newspapers. The routine drill, the labor of keeping the station and the boats and outfit bright and clean and ready for business, and the lonely night patrol of the silent beach, constitute the bulk of the men's work. But, when the lookout or the patrol see the soaring rockets or the mad danger flare to the seaward, then strenuous times follow. There are no visible fang-like rocks to show where the danger lies. The warning lights, the known position on the chart, the tumultuous white water alone tell of the proximity of danger and the sand, a few feet down does the rest: and the rest is often rest indeed for both ship and men.

Cape Hatteras, and its outlying shoals, constitute one of the most widely known,—and as widely dreaded,—points of danger to the seafarer in the world. Up and down the coast ply the schooners and cargo boats, the lumber vessels and fruiters; all the heterogeneous mass of vessels of every conceivable size and rig to which is confined the vast volume of traffic always flowing backwards and forwards from north to south and south to north along our eastern seaboard, and from the perils of this point the best of protection must be given it. With lighthouse on shore and lightship at sea it would seem that the protection now given were sufficient but such is not the case. There is building now in a northern shipyard the great caisson that is to form the foundation for another lighthouse, one that will be unique of its kind. This caisson is more than a hundred feet in diameter and eighty feet high and its bottom when sunk in the sands of the outer Diamond shoals to a depth of about twenty-six feet, will carry the weight of the caisson itself, with its load of concrete, and, above that a steel tower rising above the surface of the water for a hundred and fifty feet more. It is a daring project* but the faith of the inventor and builder is such that he has agreed to build and equip the structure and keep it in operation at his own risk for a period covering several years before receiving any pay for the work.

Conditions here are peculiar. The set of the tides up and down the coast with the incessant fight of wind against tide, the proximity of the north-easterly flowing current of the Gulf Stream and the long reach of dangerous shoal all tend to create both water and atmospheric disturbances dangerous to shipping. The gales of Hatteras are known and dreaded everywhere among seafarers. They are frequent and fierce during the stormy period of the year and woe to the vessel caught unprepared or undermanned on a lee shore here.

A curious feature connected with the navigation around this point is that with a wind from about south-east to south-west sailing vessels bound south cannot round the Cape. A strong current—possibly an offshoot from the Gulf Stream—sweeps across and around the shoals in a north-easterly direction and so strong is it that a sailing vessel cannot beat against it. Hence, in the summer season when the prevailing winds are southerly, south bound craft often collect north of the Cape in numbers awaiting

* The project was not successful.

a change in the wind. One day last July from the top of the lighthouse I counted twenty-one sailing vessels, all of them three and four master schooners, beating back and forth unable to get around the point of the shoals. A friend had counted fifty-three one day a month or so previous to this and a man connected with the life saving service told me that in August of the previous year, when the wind had remained southerly for twenty-six consecutive days, he counted no less than a hundred and five vessels weather-bound north of the Cape.

The Cape Hatteras lighthouse is a hundred and ninety feet from ground level to focal plane, and ground level is, officially, two feet above sea level. The spiral stairway up which one tramps to reach the lookout gallery is said to be composed of three hundred and twenty steps. I never counted them but I think none were missing any time I climbed the tower.

On both the Diamond and the Outer Shoals the minimum depth of water is some four or five feet, but that depth only prevails over very restricted areas. Much of the shoal is, however, inside the three fathom curve but, between the two main areas are several narrow and tortuous channels carrying four fathoms or more. But they are not often used except by shallow draft vessels in settled calm weather. The danger is too great.

Like all sand promontories the point of the Cape is always moving. An old wreck, imbedded deep in the sand and showing only the stumps of her masts and bowsprit and the rusty skeletons of what were once her chain plates and dead eyes, is now a quarter of a mile or more inland. Twenty years ago she is said to have lain in the water where she struck or drifted ashore, the land now outside of her having been built up since by the action of the wind and the waves. A resident told me that he owned the copper that still remained on the bottom, having bought it as it stood at the "vendue" or wreck sale. I don't think anyone is likely to steal it from him.

This is strictly a maritime community. Dare County, North Carolina, of which the cape and its surroundings are a part, consists of a peninsula on the mainland, Roanoke Island,—the scene of the first Anglo-Saxon settlement in America—and the strip of "banks" from Kittyhawk Bay on the north down to Hatteras Inlet to the south and west. Seventy miles long is this strip, mostly sand beach and dune with marsh on the side next to the sound. This long, narrow ribbon of barrier between sound and ocean is broken up into islands by Oregon, New and Hatteras Inlets and is peopled entirely by fishermen and men in the Government Life Saving and Lighthouse service. I might except the proprietors of the several general stores but their living comes indirectly, and often much of it directly, from fishing and oystering too. My genial friend, Doctor J. J. Davis,* the only physician for twenty-five miles one way and fifty the other, might be thought an exception but even he fishes a little between professional calls in this very healthy community.

Up the beach, towards Kittyhawk and the Kill Devil Hills, some sizable bodies of woods still exist but below Oregon Inlet hardly any tree growth is now left until the Cape is reached, the steady, remorseless march of the moving sand having gradually killed it out. But, right at the Cape, the shore line turns abruptly to the westward and here, beginning with a width of three miles, the banks narrow down to less than a mile wide some six miles away, the greater part of this triangular area being still in a fair growth of original woods. Of course there are the clearings surrounding the houses of the inhabitants and their patches of garden, these being mostly on the sound side. This is the village of Buxton, a straggling settlement some two or three miles in length. It is joined at its western end by the village of Frisco or Trent, a similar settlement in every way. I have no data but suppose that probably four or five hundred people live in these two neighborhoods. By the way, most of the post offices up and down the banks hereabouts have two names, one the old name by which everybody knows and calls them and the other made in Washington, I suppose, and mostly used in directing letters. Thus, Frisco was once Trent; Avon was and still mostly remains Kinnekeet; and Salvo is yet Chicomicomico to everybody around, unless he is letter writing. The woods above mentioned are bordered on the sound side by a strip of marsh

* Father of Harry T. Davis, present Director of the State Museum.

and on the ocean side by a bare sand beach, both of varying widths. The woodland between consists of a series of ridges alternating with long shallow irregular fresh water ponds, more or less filled with a sedgy growth and locally known as sedges. In these woods live the deer, often lying up in the daytime on small islands in the sedge. By reason of the conformity of the country, the hunting of them is attended with many difficulties. And into these ponds at night come the Black Duck and Mallard but they have been shot so much during the flight, that they now come in late and go out early, a practice much to be commended.

The woodland growth has a scattering—a good scattering—of fair sized pine, lots of holly, and live oak and yopon, a great deal of dogwood in places and a mixed undergrowth, with here and there patches of dwarf palmetto. All around the sedges are a dense growth of bay and myrtle. In the spring, when the dogwood is in bloom, the woods are beautiful beyond compare. Twisting avenues and straight reaches, spots of sun and shade and the wood roads lined with dense banks of the snowy blossoms combine to make a fascinating picture indeed. In winter, too, the woods are remarkably attractive, so much of the growth being evergreen. But at this season of the year one naturally turns to the water if one has an ounce of sporting blood in one's veins, for the wildfowl are there waiting.

Pamlico Sound, as might be expected, is shoal all over, attaining nowhere a depth of more than twenty-four feet and, in the main body of the sound, the depth is very even, most of it running from sixteen to twenty-one feet. Of course it shoals very much along the shores and on these broad shallows thousands, perhaps millions, of geese and brant and ducks live their winter life. I doubt if any locality in the eastern States harbors greater numbers of brant and geese than do the shoals for twenty-five miles each way inside the banks from Cape Hatteras.

In this region four-wheeled vehicles are practically unknown, the only exceptions being the boat wagons at the Life Saving stations. These are used for hauling the heavy lifeboats from their houses down to the water's edge and are fitted with six inch tires to provide broad bearing surfaces on the loose sand over which they have to run. Two wheel "beach carts" are the usual type of general purpose vehicle. This cart consists of a pair of rather high wheels, a flat platform or shallow box body and a pair of shafts—simplicity personified. The pleasure and social type is a sort of road cart, with springs and seat but, in this sort of country, all wheels must be broad tired and no exception is made in this case. There is no speedway near at hand and the sand is always present and always deep.

A few old windmills still exist in the region of the Cape. The one at Buxton went down in a blow last October and the only one still in active service is a few miles up the beach at Kinnekeet.

A wireless telegraph station is in operation not far from the lighthouse with a skeleton tower exceeding that of the lighthouse in height. The list of vessels kept at the station with which communication can be had is quite a long one and is continually being enlarged. When messages are being sent the din inside the sending room is frightful and the whole atmosphere seems to vibrate to the shock of the discharge. It gives one the impression of irresistible, deadly force and I am told that these powerful electrical waves turned loose in the atmosphere induce such activity in the telephone wire hereabouts as to make them utterly useless while the sending is going on.

As stated before, the official name for the post office for the region around the Cape is Buxton, Hatteras post office being near the inlet of the same name ten miles to the westward. Locally, though, it is always called "The Cape."

A product of this part of the world that is but little known and which is mostly consumed locally is yopon tea. The leaves of the yopon (*Ilex vomitoria*) still attached to the smaller twigs are chopped up small, put through a sweating process under artificial heat, dried and packed in sacks for storage and subsequent sale. The regular price is twenty-five cents a bushel, and, with people who have not acquired the habit, a bushel goes a long way.

Deer, raccoon, possum and gray squirrel are the principal animals of these Hatteras woods. No bear, foxes or wildcat occur, nor does our friend Bob-White make his home here.

In the summertime the breeding gulls and terns occupy certain shoals and bare "lumps" out in the sound and now that the protective laws are being enforced their numbers are rapidly increasing. Herons of various kinds nest in the woods; and so also do a pair or two of Bald Eagles and, last summer, several good sized flocks of Brown Pelicans enlivened some of the nearby reefs and sandy islands.

Two features connecting with the sailing of the fishing skiffs used hereabouts are new to me. One is that of using one of the crew as shifting ballast. A plank is run out over the side, the inner end caught under the lee wash boards while on the outer end, with legs dangling over the water, sits the man acting as ballast; and this not in racing, mind you, but in everyday sailing. The other is the practice of "nodding" as I heard it called. In moderate weather when the skiff is only lightly gliding along, one man will stand up alongside the centerboard, on the weather side and, facing outward, will steadily rock sidewise from one foot to the other with the idea that it makes the boat sail faster. And perhaps it does.

Putting the finishing touches on the specimen of the Glassy Ibis. This picture was made in 1940. (*N. C. State Museum*)

A more formal portrait of the North Carolina naturalist in his later years, April, 1937.

The North Carolina State Fair in the 1890's*

MIGHTY FEW OF MY READERS will have any recollection of the old-time State Fair of forty and more years ago, and it may be that some comparison between now and then will prove of interest.

Two of the impressive features of forty-odd years ago were the deep red mud or the unspeakable red dust, according to the weather, and the tented barrooms where the mud could be forgotten or the dust washed from one's throat, as the case might be.

* H. H. Brimley, in common with many of us, got a huge kick out of fairs. He had an especially soft spot in his heart for the North Carolina State Fair since it was at the Raleigh Centennial Exposition in 1885 that he first exhibited his mounted specimens of native birds and mammals. His brief description of the old time fair of the 1890's which was published in the *Agricultural Review* (N. C. State Dept. Agriculture), September 25, 1931, may not be out of place here.

Of course, the agricultural exhibitor from a distance, who started from home several days in advance of the Fair, brought his week's nourishment with him, at times mainly in the form of several jugs of cawn licker, which were hidden away in the back of his untidy exhibit or in the hay of the so-called stable where he parked his team. Paper cups were unknown then and glasses too easy to break, so the nourishment was usually inhaled through the medium of a gourd or direct from the neck of the jug.

The three-card monte man worked back of the old grand stand or around the stables, as it was felt that the conventionalities should be observed. But the man with the three walnut shells and the little pea, who operated on a small folding platform, or table, that was suspended by a string around his neck, made his scientific demonstration of how "the quickness of the hand deceives the eye" almost anywhere on the grounds. He and his cappers were an important part of the Fair, as the visitor in those days insisted on his simple and innocent amusements.

It goes without saying that the ticket sellers at the side shows were short-change artists, and some of them were post-graduates in their manly art. The strong-lunged vendor of oroide rolled gold jewelry was on hand, and the man who sold little cubes of common laundry soap as the Great and Only Original and Certain Remover of Grease Spots from Clothing—"only twenty-five cents, one quarter of a dollar"—did a thriving trade.

My impression now is that the fat woman was fatter and the living skeleton leaner than they are now, but perhaps the rosy glow of distance tends to warp my judgment.

An agricultural exhibit was judged by the size of the biggest "punkin" or the number of pieces in a crazy quilt. An extra large gourd, or a carrot with two legs, always excited admiration and, of course, an eight-legged pig in a fruit jar was the belle of the ball!

The horse races were sometimes a little bit rough in character. Some of the drivers seemed to be out to win—irrespective! And I've seen some rather dirty driving on that old track. But they had the popular appeal, all the same, though the average spectator never felt sure that the best horse won. Pre-arrangement was openly hinted at!

The only exhibit building was the old Floral Hall, which most of you remember as a very secondary and unimposing exhibit building on the late Fair Grounds. But who cared about exhibits so long as the barrooms were open, the fat lady on exhibition, and the shell games in full blast!

Most of the visitors reached the grounds by train, those from a distance coming on excursion trains and the Raleigh people on shuttle trains that operated at frequent intervals between town and the platform alongside the Fair spur track just across the road from the main entrance gate. One-horse hacks—and two-horse conveyances for those more aristocratically inclined —added to the transportation facilities. Automobiles were, of course, still in the future, and the little city street cars, that were pulled by mules about the size of jack-rabbits, stayed close around the center of town. The Fair Grounds were way out in the country in those good old days.

Quite a step, isn't it, from then to now!

PART TWO

Hunting and Fishing

EDITOR'S NOTE

The following selections are a few of the dozens of stories and accounts of hunting and fishing in eastern North Carolina, many of which were written for and published in sporting magazines. Brimley had a way of capturing the atmosphere of the occasion and of weaving into the narrative many of his personal observations on habits of the game in question. For these reasons, his stories are of lasting interest and well worth reprinting here.

People in general are rather sharply divided when it comes to hunting and fishing; either they are crazy about it or they care nothing for it. The following selections, however, I believe will interest anyone, hunting enthusiast or not. The non-sportsman will be particularly impressed with the fact that, when the methods are fair and "sporting," comparatively few animals or fish are actually bagged, the ones that get away being both numerous and large! This is as it should be. The long hikes through country unspoiled by man, the chance to get away from petty troubles of complex modern civilization, the matching of wits with cunning wild kindred, the hearty meal cooked in the open, and the companionship around the campfire are things which appeal to the real sportsman and outdoorman more than the actual game obtained. Of course, the hunter or fisherman is disappointed when he comes back empty-handed; partly, at least, because his friends expect him to have something to show for the trip besides his own mental and physical rejuvenation. Nevertheless, even the unsuccessful trip is a success to the true sportsman if he be also a nature lover. Such a man was H. H. Brimley.

Bill's Christmas Bear[*]

No, it didn't happen to me. Usually, I am glad that it did not; at other times—well, it all depends on the frame of mind I happen to be in at the time. Bill makes light of it now, but at the time of the telling—Christmas night—he was a bit shaky still and needed the drink that was handed to him when he arrived at camp. And he sure did look a sight.

I was not there when he left camp on the morning of Christmas Eve, or he would not have been alone on the trip. I missed the night train and arrived after Bill had left, taking my little canvas canoe with him. That's a nice little boat of mine, by the way. I built her myself, and she works well under both sail and paddle and I may have something more to say about that ship in another article. I noticed that Bill had taken two paddles with him, a very wise precaution when one is alone. Sometimes a paddle will drop overboard—and the need of this precaution is proved right there.

* Based on a story written for the *Charlotte Daily Observer* about 1910.

Here is the story as Bill told it, as nearly as possible in his own words:

I crossed Smith Lake all right and made the carry across to Broad Lake: It took me two trips; one for the canoe and another for the outfit. I had, as you know, frying pan and coffee pot, grub for two or three days, blanket, and my usual hunting things, as rifle, hatchet, hunting knife and compass.

Once launched on Broad Lake I felt all right. There was enough wind from the northward to make the paddling good, muscle-forming work though not enough to kick up much of a sea. So I made straight across to that place on the north shore where the swamp and pocoson come together—where we have so often before talked of taking a hunt. That made it a good deal shorter than hugging the shore line, which would have been necessary had the lake been a little rougher, or the wind from the westward.

The wind being from a little west of north—off shore—I selected a camping place on a little dry ridge close to the water. I carried the duffle ashore, picked out a place to set up the canoe as a wind-break later on, and made a snug little camp. As there was plenty of time—it was an hour before noon when I landed —I packed in a supply of firewood sufficient for the two nights I expected to be out, and arranged everything handy, so as to be able to hunt as late in the evening as I could see my rifle sights. Then I built up a small cooking fire, boiled the coffee, and had dinner, and after a quiet smoke and an hour's rest I was ready for the afternoon's hunt. After putting out the fire I took the canoe and paddled along shore towards the open pocoson, and landed to look for sign. But, before leaving my camp, I had tied a handkerchief on a bush at the extreme end of the point below which the camp lay, as the shore line is densely wooded and a fellow needs some kind of a landmark to find any particular place after dark. But you fellows know how it is all around the lake, so I needn't explain any further.

Well! There's game out there, all right. You know we hardly ever hunt that far away from headquarters, and the dogs scarcely ever follow a deer out there. So the place is practically undisturbed. There was deer sign a plenty, regular paths through the pocoson where it was thick, and scattering sign everywhere. And I saw some bear tracks that looked not older than the night before.

I wandered around investigating until about mid-afternoon looking for a good place to "set," and finally found one that suited me all right. It was a nice open place, well sheltered from the wind—which was rather keen—and with several game paths coming together nearby. I killed a small buck about an hour by sun, having seen a much larger one that I did not get a shot at. The biggest one always gets away, you know. I managed to drag and pack my buck to the canoe, and soon had it back at the camping place. Not wishing to have my night's rest disturbed by every prowling beast that might be attracted by the smell of blood, I took it off a hundred yards or so along the shore for butchering. After bending down a good limber sapling, I tied the buck's head to that and then, by means of a couple of forked poles, I hoisted the carcass high enough for comfort in dressing. That done, it was easy enough by moving one of the poles in at a time, to hoist the body out of the reach of night prowlers. I then rubbed my hands and my hunting coat all over the poles and the sapling so that the man-scent would keep any stray coon from climbing after a meal, and transferred the entrails to a sack and the sack to the canoe. This was to be used as a drag bait for bear on the morrow, which would be Christmas Day.

The night passed quietly, though it was a powerful long one. I had a good fire, and sat and smoked and fed the fire until too dead sleepy to keep it up any longer. Then, under the lee of the turned-up canoe, on a good soft bed of dry leaves from the woods and wire grass from the open ground, I rolled the blanket around me and turned in.

By daylight I had a small cooking fire drawn out from the re-mainder of the night's camp fire and soon had the coffee boiling, some slices of deer liver and pork fried together, and half a dozen cold biscuits fried in the pork and liver gravy. That was a good Christmas breakfast, let me tell you. I had forgotten to hang up my stockings the night before (I had slept in them, to tell the plain truth) so there were no useless presents to rave over and lie about. But the total absence of all those features that we usually associate with Christmas morning certainly did give me a feeling that something human and kindly was missing from my surroundings.

After washing the dishes I strolled over to look at my buck, which I found, as I expected, all right and undisturbed. Being in a nice, cool, shady spot, it was left hanging there for the present.

It being evident to me that there was a man's work ahead of me in dragging that bunch of "haslets" through the swamp, I took things easily for an hour or two. The bed was re-made, the windbreak added to, and a sort of shelter built over the bed to keep off the falling dew.

The night before I had taken the precaution of soaking the sack containing the deer's innards in the blood of the animal when I dressed it, as I wanted a good strong trail to result from the drag. The wind was still northerly, which was off shore for this side of the lake. It was plain, therefore, that the bait would have to be taken well back into the swamp, to windward of any trails a wandering bear might use. I had my machete along, one of those long, sword-like knives of the tropical Spanish-American countries that serve equally well for cutting sugar cane, carving a course through the dense tropical jungles, or removing the head of a troublesome enemy. And it is *the* tool for making a passage through our eastern swamps, cane brakes and pocosons, with their tangle of fetter bush and bamboo brier. And so it proved that day.

I struck out, towing the drag astern at the end of a six-foot cord, and headed back into the swamp almost directly away from the lake. My course lay about north-east, and I dragged that tempting bait a matter of more than a mile before turning off to the westward. Then another mile or so in that direction, with the third leg of the course about southerly and back to the lake shore. I judged the total distance covered to be between three and four miles—and it was heart-breaking work at times. The cover was so thick in places—even though the most open were selected—as to necessitate a constant use of the machete, and it took a good three hours to make the round. But fresh bear sign was seen in several places and conditions looked good for one finding the trail of the drag—and following it up. Every now and then I would stop and trample on the sack, both with the idea of keeping the scent of fresh deer meat on my boots as well as to start a renewed flow of the tempting juices through the pores of the sack.

When the shore was finally reached it proved to be at a point nearly half a mile to the westward of the camp. So, after hanging up the drag well above ground, and taking a short rest, I headed back to the camp after the canoe, following the game trail that runs all around the lake, usually pretty close to the water's edge. The canoe was brought to where I intended to "set," drawn up on shore, and the expectant wait began.

I had a fairly open place to shoot in—if game came along—with heavy thickets and some down timber just to the eastward of the place. It was about two thirty in the afternoon when things were ready for business; there was a good sized dead log for a seat, the wind was right, and the wait promised to be a most welcome rest after the arduous work of making the trail.

The usual sights and sounds of the swamp were in evidence. Squirrels chattered and ran all around me, great owls hooted back in the swamp and the log-cocks yelled and hammered in the still evening air.

A fellow's thoughts at such a time and among such surroundings are likely to cover a wide ground, apart from the business at hand. I know mine did. I thought of my remoteness from help in case of accident, of the total incapacity of certain "street bred" friends of mine for understanding this kind of enjoyment, and of another lake I know, where the clear waters lap a clean, sandy shore and where the great bald eagles nest in the nearby swamp. Then I got to watching the squirrels feeding on the ground—on the fallen gum berries, I think.

Listen! Something—some large body was moving back there in the thickets—and in a moment every sense was on the alert.

I fingered my rifle—a twenty-five automatic Remington—to see that the safety was off, and then drew back the bolt enough to make sure that a cartridge was in the chamber. Another touch of the finger told me that the rear sight—a flexible peep—was in place, and I felt ready and prepared.

The rustling and crashing through the bushes was gradually drawing nearer, every now and then stopping, and then coming on again. But the animal—I was certain by this time that it was a bear—seemed uneasy and uncertain, and was not following the trail I had made but was circling about and trying to keep to leeward of it all the time, as the trail here ran almost across the wind. This I had not bargained for, and the result was that the beast came within easy shooting distance but still remained out of sight in the dense growth to the eastward of where I was standing—as I had come to my feet at the first sound.

Finally, I saw its head, but it was gone again before I had time to shoot. He evidently had not seen me yet but he had my scent mixed up with the scent of the drag, and it made him particularly shy and wary.

I began to fear I was not going to get a shot after all, when again the head suddenly appeared through the bushes, and I caught a quick sight and fired. There was a crash as the bear dropped—and all was still again. With finger on trigger I waited a full minute, it seemed to me—and then went carefully forward into the thicket. There lay my bear, and a big one he was, too. He was perfectly still and looked limp and as dead as a door nail, and the blood still oozing through the thick fur on the top of his head showed that the bullet had gone true. Proud, was I? Well, yes and then some.

After a moment's hesitation I stooped through the bushes and briers and touched him with my foot. A quiver or two ran through his massive body—which I took to be involuntary muscular movement—and then I placed my foot on his head. Suddenly his whole body gave a great heave, and with a convulsive effort he raised his great head—and saw me. I tried to jump back to get room to shoot. My foot caught in a brier and I stumbled back against a tangle of briers and bushes in such a position that

I could neither bring up my rifle in a position from which to shoot, nor get out of the bear's way. Dazed from the glancing bullet—as I later found it to be—and half blinded by the blood that had covered one eye, he came to his feet and lurched right at me. I thought then—and one thinks quickly under such conditions—that it was a purposeful and revengeful attack, directed intelligently at his enemy. But cooler reasoning now makes me believe it to have been purely accidental that he came my way. But come he did. In a moment I was down, down through the thorny, bushy tangle, with the great brute—now realizing that he had an enemy at his mercy—on top, and I so tangled up and pressed down as to be almost helpless. He was still partly dazed from the impact of the high power bullet, I think, or he would either have made short work of me then and there, or he would have taken to his heels at once. But the situation was serious enough and it makes my flesh creep even now to think of it.

I had fallen partly on my right side and the rifle had dropped from my hands as I went down, but my right hand was partly free. The great head of the brute was over my face, and I could feel the drip of saliva and blood as he mumbled and mouthed over my head. Instinctively my left arm went up to cover and protect my face, and he grabbed that in his jaws, while one front paw raked down my breast, reaching the meat in places.

Now, in my belt, the four things that always hang therefrom when hunting have each a particular place, and I knew that my hunting knife was on the left side towards the front, which was uppermost as I was lying. A quick movement of my right hand grasped its handle and it cleared the sheath readily, and in a moment I had it up to the guard in his side. He chewed harder on my arm and his powerful claws raked me again. But, by this time I was mad too, baresark mad, and again and again I drove that steel five-inch blade in between his ribs. It seemed hours, but was in reality hardly minutes, before the frothing jaws slipped off my arm and the great hairy body relaxed and slowly subsided alongside of mine. Then I crawled to my feet, only to sink back again in a weak, dazed condition—as I was about all in, and for a few moments all physical and nervous force seemed to have left me. I felt then as if he had got me as thoroughly as I him.

But, with returning breath and slower heart-beats, I got myself together a little and began to take stock of my injuries. Strange to say I was almost unhurt. The scratches on my chest amounted to nothing and the three or four thicknesses of heavy winter clothing on my arm, with a Duxbak hunting coat over all, had protected it to such an extent that only a few bruises and one or two unimportant tooth punctures showed there. But I was a sight for Gods and men! The upper parts of my clothing were torn to shreds, and I was covered with blood—bear's blood—from the waist up. Had I had any with me, a good, stiff drink of whiskey would have been worth a dollar a drop about then. But I had only lake water handy—and that a hundred yards away. Picking up my rifle I staggered over to the lake and drank and washed, and then drank some more.

But I was all unstrung, and then and there I decided that this lonely swamp was no place for mother's fair-haired boy to spend another night in alone. So I bundled into the canoe—it was now about four in the afternoon—and hit the high places for this good old camp and some human company, and here I am. The bear and the buck and the camp outfit are where I left them, and you fellows can go over there with me in the morning and get out the game and see where it all happened. Thanks, I *will* take another.

That is Bill's story. The next day three of us, with Bill to guide us to the place, went over, and every mark around where the bear lay dead tended to show that the episode had not been exaggerated. We brought out the game—and Bill's camp outfit—and he has been the hero of camp ever since. And I here repeat what I said at the beginning, that I am usually glad that it didn't happen to me, though, sometimes—Well! we'll let it go at that. And I have not yet killed a bear!

What Will a Deer Do? [*]

T HE WHITE-TAILED DEER is a long way from becoming extinct in many sections of the eastern part of this state. It occurs in some numbers in forty or more counties of the coastal plain area, and in possibly two-thirds of these counties it may be regarded as more or less plentiful.

The hunting of this elusive animal carries with it thrills that are not found in the following of any other game bird or animal, and in this short paper I shall endeavor to present some characteristics of the White-tailed Deer, together with incidents connected with its hunting.

One of the great attractions of deer hunting is the uncertainty as to what action an individual deer will take under given conditions. I have hunted deer in eastern North Carolina every season for more than twenty-five years—with some degree of success—and my experience of the actions of the animal when hunted is that it usually does the unexpected.

[*] Unpublished manuscript written about 1942.

But of one thing you may be perfectly sure, this being that the instant a moving deer catches the taint of fresh human scent it whirls away down wind, goes into high gear, and steps hard on the gas.

A peculiar habit in which our deer occasionally indulge is the "crawl" act. On two of the three times that this has been performed under my observation, the deer escaped without affording me an opportunity to shoot, but on the third experience, when the crawl was made through water averaging about nine inches deep, I was enabled to note the small, bushy island on which the animal hid, and move over and jump him within easy range. His mounted head is now in my personal collection.

This act of crawling is usually performed when the deer, after traversing more or less brushy territory, reaches a more open place in which grass, dead fern or other low growth offer the only hiding medium. The deer may then drop down on its belly and worm its way through the low vegetation until other territory affording better hiding is reached. And it is truly amazing how an animal weighing from 75 to 150 pounds can traverse a stretch that would hardly hide a rabbit, without exposing its presence to the watchful hunter. But deer are wily animals and are keen to take advantage of every opportunity of escaping their enemies.

All members of the deer family shed their antlers every year. In this region, the shedding is usually carried out in February, the exact date varying with the age and condition of the individual. Soon after the antlers have been dropped, the new ones start growing from the scars left by those that have been discarded, and they attain their full growth in about five months. While growing, the horns are soft, full of blood-vessels, and very susceptible of injury, and they are covered with a thick growth of soft, short hair, usually known as "velvet." As soon as the growth is completed, the connecting blood-vessels are shut off from the horn by the formation of the "burr," a bony ring that encircles each antler near its base. The horns then become dead bone and the velvet begins to peel off; and the bucks aid Nature in cleaning the horns by rubbing them against bushes and small saplings. Before the mating season starts in early October, the antlers are clean, and clear of the velvet, and the prongs show highly polished tips; and they are then ready for use in the fighting in which the bucks are likely to engage at this season.

In eastern North Carolina, the fawns are, in general, born in May or early June. They are of a reddish brown color thickly spotted with white, the spots being retained for about four months. By October, or earlier, the fawns have lost their spots, and the reddish color of the body-hair has been replaced by a gray winter-coat similar in color to the winter-pelage of the adult deer. The summer-coat of the adults is a reddish-brown.

Fawns of a few months old are graceful and beautiful creatures and quite able to take care of themselves in the woods.

During the first winter, the male fawns develop small nubbins in the places where the antlers will grow later on. The following year sees these nubbins grown into spikes, with no forks, and during this period these youngsters are known as "spike-horn" or "peg-horn" bucks. These spikes are shed the following February, or thereabouts, the next year's growth usually showing two points to each antler. Normally, another point is added each year until four or five are shown on each side, but this is by no means an invariable rule.

Five or six years ago, I was shown by the owner of a herd of captive deer, in Wayne County, the shed antlers of the buck for a period of five years. The first year's horns consisted of the usual pair of single-pointed spikes, but—much to my surprise —those of the second year had four points to each antler, and those of the three succeeding years each carried four points to the horn. Each set showed an increase in size over that of the preceding year, but there was no increase in the number of points. Of course, the peculiar feature of the exhibit was the jump from one point to four points in one season.

Up to about seven years of age the antlers usually come larger each year. After that, though the buck itself may continue to increase in size and weight, the horns decrease yearly until an old and very large buck often carries a poor set of antlers. This characteristic is common to most of the members of the deer family.

The White-tailed Deer is a fine swimmer. I do not mean by this statement that it is at home in the water in a way comparable to the otter, beaver, or muskrat, but that a long swim in cold water may be taken voluntarily at any time.

Several winters ago, on a very cold day, I was in a duck-blind on New River, in Onslow County, the blind being situated perhaps a hundred or a hundred and fifty yards from shore. Dogs were running in the woods in the rear of my blind, and I finally saw the buck they were following come down the steep bank and take to the water. Now, this deer could have very easily thrown the dogs off his scent by wading along in the shallow water parallel to the shore for two or three hundred yards and again entering the woods. But he seemed to be out for a swim.

He waded out until swimming depth was reached and then struck out directly off-shore as if intending to swim across the river, which was approximately two and a half miles wide at this point. But when five or six hundred yards from shore, he altered his course to the down-river direction and headed for a distant promontory known as Ward's Point and, when last seen, he was still heading directly for that objective. This was a deliberate voluntary swim of about two miles in very cold water on a very cold day.

About sunrise of another cold morning I was paddling my canoe up Cowhead Creek on my way to an outlying deer-stand, taking this means of reaching it in order to avoid a long, tedious walk. No breeze was stirring, and I was moving the canoe along in almost perfect silence.

Suddenly, from around a bend just ahead of the boat, came a deer, leisurely swimming down the middle of the creek. He was a big buck, with the finest head of horns I have ever seen on a live deer, and he evidently regarded the boat and me as a harmless drifting log. The canoe slowly drifted forward, and I remained perfectly motionless until the deer was within about thirty feet—when I reached for my rifle. Instantly, he caught the movement and turned and headed for shore, the back of his great neck and shoulders rising high as he plowed through the water.

Now, it is not only illegal to kill a deer in the water, but it is distinctly unethical and wrong, as a swimming deer has no chance of escape whatever from a man in a boat, so I picked the open place on the bank of the creek on which I expected him to land and sat with finger on trigger awaiting the opportune moment. And how I did crave those magnificent antlers for the wall of my den.

But the unexpected happened, as usual. A tiny depression in the line of bank, that I had overlooked, was overhung with bushes, and he took the land completely out of my sight, though not more than twenty yards away. I saw the bushes shake as his feet struck firm ground and he leaped forward, and I sent a random bullet into the thicket. But I haven't seen that big buck since the overhanging bushes hid him.

This wily old buck had evidently been roaming the woods during the night and was on his way back to the thickets in which he expected to lie up for the day. His sense, instinct, and experience had led him to take to the water for a good part of his journey, so that any enemies that might pick up the devious trail of his nocturnal wanderings would be thrown off his track where it entered the water. No dogs were after him and every evidence showed that he was taking this ice-cold morning bath for his own protection and of his own volition.

When run by hounds, a deer will show a wonderful cunning in throwing off the dogs, often successfully in the case of young, inexperienced hounds. A weaving back and forth in a tangle of bushes and briers that the deer leaps easily over, but which the dogs have to creep through, is often adapted. Usually, a straight-away run follows, an old buck often returning for a distance on the back trail and then leaping far off to one side. Reaching the place at which the deer turned back, the dogs are at fault. A young dog will soon give up when he finds that the trail has ended in a way that can only be accounted for—to his inexperienced mind—by the deer having gone up in the air, or out of existence. Not so an experienced deer hound, however. He follows back on a line parallel with the original trail, first on one side and then on the other until he reaches the place where the deer made his getaway to one side. But it is a great gain in time and distance to the deer, and that much extra work and worry to the dogs.

Eventually, however, if all the wiles of the quarry fail to throw off the dogs, the deer will take to water. And here again the ways of the deer and the particular plan he will follow, neither man nor dog can foresee. Sometimes the deer will wade out on the the shallows, follow the shore line for several hundred yards, and then go back to the woods. At others he will cross a stream, either narrow or wide—it makes but little difference to him— directly. Or, he may swim down wind in the stream for half a mile or more and then take land again on either side. The great number and variety of creeks, rivers and lakes in eastern North Carolina is one of the prime factors in keeping up our supply of native deer.

There are fifty-seven varieties—methods, that is—of carrying the deer after it is killed, but there is no easy way. I remember a published photograph of a hunter in the northern woods with a big buck across his shoulders, rifle in hand—and a smile on his face. The title was: "It takes a good woodsman and a good man to trail and kill a two-hundred-pound buck, and bring him out of the woods, unassisted!" I'll say it does! And men capable of performing the feat are about as scarce as feathers on the back of a catfish!

eft, Bringing home the deer, the culmination of Mr. Brimley's favorite sport. *Right,* One-
an camp on Long Lake in the early days (about 1905). The canoe propped up by a gun
as used as a shelter for a sleeping bag. *Below left,* Mr. Brimley admiring a good catch.
elow right, Informal picture of H. H. Brimley taken by his good friend, T. Gilbert Pear-
n at Orton Pond, eastern North Carolina.

Above, A pony and road cart at Cape Hatteras, 1900-3. *Below left,* The picturesque Cape
Hatteras Lighthouse was abandoned in 1936, and a 166-foot skeleton tower was erected to
replace it. *Below right,* Dugout tree-section sweat-box for steeping yopon tea. Yopon twigs
and leaves were placed in the dugout and heated with hot rocks. (*All, N. C. State Museum.*)

Coon Hunting — As Is [*]

A<small>MONG HUNTERS</small> and fishermen there are a few—a very few—able-bodied liars, but I have sometimes thought that the coon-hunters provide more of this type of human than all other groups of hunters and fishermen combined. Of course, I may be wrong in this, but I have my doubts.

The typical coon hunter always has dogs that "ain't never been known to run nuthin' but a coon!" And here is a typical coon hunt that will illustrate what I mean.

Down in Onslow County a few years ago we used to talk about hunting coons, but the only dogs we had were trained to run nothing but deer, so one of the members of the Club from a near-by town brought a real, old-time coon hunter with him on his next visit, together with a brace of real coon hounds.

The owner of the dogs was a dyed-in-the-wool coon-hunter. He told me confidentially that he could see nothing in staying all day in a cold duck blind in the hope of killing a few measly

[*] Unpublished manuscript.

ducks, in shivering on a deer stand all the morning awaiting the deer that never came, in walking himself to death following the elusive quail, and so forth and so on. But coon-hunting was something entirely different—from his point of view. It was the very acme, grand slam and ace-in-the-hole of outdoor recreation.

Listening to the voices of the trailing dogs as one followed them quietly; then, as the trail grew hotter, following them more rapidly until they treed. And then! The rush through the bushes, over prostrate logs and everything else until the tree was reached and the coon secured!

"And just look at the coon when you've got him," he continued, "feel of his deep, soft fur, look at the handsome black markings across his face, observe the beautiful rings on his tail, etc." One might think from his description that a coon is perhaps a cross between a peacock and a bird of paradise, except that it is equipped with fur instead of feathers and with four legs in place of two. Yes, he was a coon-hunter, all right.

That night we waited until about nine o'clock before starting out, with the two hounds that had never been known to run anything but a coon, the late hour of starting being due to the widely-held opinion that the larger coons do not walk early in the night.

Only a few minutes passed before the dogs opened up, and in a few minutes, treed. And the game they had treed turned out to be one of the very common house cats that infested the Club-house.

The owner of the dogs called them several names in an unfriendly tone of voice, and again sent them out after a real coon. And it was not long before they again hit a hot trail.

This time the run was again comparatively short, and when we arrived at the spot we found the dogs baying at a small hollow close to the ground in a not-very-large tree. There was hair around the edges of the opening that was suspiciously like rabbit fur, and after procuring a slender pole and poking it up the hollow until the game was reached, a twisting movement of the pole soon engaged it with the fur of the animal—and a marsh rabbit was brought to light. Two specimens run and treed, and no coon, so far.

The dogs were again reprimanded and again turned loose in search of what we supposed them to be after.

They struck a cold trail this time, which gradually warmed up until they were going loud and strong.

"That's a ole he-coon, this time; I kin tell by the long ways he's a-carrying them dawgs," remarked the dogs' owner. "They'll soon hev him treed, now."

But alack and alas, the consensus of the opinion of the crowd was that the hounds were following a fox or a deer, and finally the hunter's horn brought them back to heel.

Somehow, conversation seemed to lag after this third fiasco of the dogs that "wouldn't never run nuthin' but a coon," but hope seemed to be springing eternal in the human breast, and the hounds were given another opportunity to live up to their reputations.

They did a little better this time by treeing a possum in a stump hole, but the coons we were after seemed perfectly able to elude even these experienced and well-trained hounds.

The night was dragging along by this time, but it was decided that one more trial be made in an effort to have a real ring-tailed coon to take back to the Club-house, we being all wet to the skin, anyway, by working through the bushes that were dripping under a heavy dew.

It was some time before another trail was struck, but the dogs took it hot-foot when they did strike it, and they soon treed, again in a stump-hole. But long before we could get to the dogs we knew what they had treed. The damp air seemed almost saturated with the odor that only a skunk can produce.

The stump hole was in a dense thicket, with lots of smilax briers interlaced among the bushes, but we finally secured the game—and turned our way wearily homeward. And, since that experience, I have always fought shy of a man who declares that "them dawgs uv mine ain't never been known to run nuthin' but a coon!"

However, all coon hunting is not like that just described. One night, in these same Onslow County woods, the dogs treed in the swamp while we—the hunters—were off on a ridge some little distance away. We piled off to the swamp, and found that the coon had picked a particularly rough place for his stand. Every man in the party of seven found what he thought was the easiest way into the swamp, but all made slow progress to the tree. In one place, for thirty or forty feet, my feet didn't touch the ground, progress being made by climbing and crawling over a mass of down fetterbushes, miscellaneous swamp-growth, and briers, some dead and some alive, that blocked the way. Finally, however, all reached the place where the dogs were holding forth. And there, up a small bay tree and not more than fifteen feet above the ground, was the coon.

Nearly every man in the party carried a flash-light, and the coon looked very peaceful and harmless in the rays of the electric torches, so much so, in fact, that the one gun in the party was not brought into play.

The dogs were wild at seeing the coon so near and yet so far out of reach, so one of the party started shaking the sapling to get the coon down and give the dogs an opportunity to show their prowess as coon-fighters.

The animal showed no sign of fear of either dogs or men. He quietly descended the tree as the rays of the flash-lights followed him down, and leaped into a thick bush at the foot of the bay tree.

The dogs rushed in, full of fight, and a grand scrap seemed a certainty. A moment or two passed; the dogs seemed unable to find their quarry; then a loud splash signified that the coon had eluded the dogs and taken to the creek, which was only a few feet away without our realizing its proximity. Personally, I was not particularly sorry that this coon got away. It would have been little short of murder to have shot him out of the tree at such close quarters. And the dogs had their chance!

Coon hunting in these eastern swamps is a he-man's job. The coons know the rough places, almost impenetrable thickets and water-logged swamps, and they use their knowledge often to the confusion of the hunters. I well remember one of the roughest of these trips.

We were trying a place across the creek from the Club-house, and the fog was so dense that we had to cross the creek—a trip of perhaps three-eighths of a mile—by compass, once the lights of the house faded away in the fog.

The dogs soon struck a trail, and treed in a big swamp. The fog was equivalent to a light rain in saturating the undergrowth, and we started wet—and remained wet until we got back to the house about three the next morning.

Into the swamp we went, every man for himself but all headed for the baying dogs.

This was a real swamp. Plenty of big gums, cypress and swamp maple, and not any places that were free of undergrowth, to say nothing of the abundance of smilax briers. There was water, and there were holes. One foot would sink into a water hole until the tops of our hip-boots were flooded. The next step might be on a tussock above the water-line—and then a fallen log as likely as not would trip the unlucky hunter completely.

This kind of going is hard, particularly when one adds the well-thorned hanging briers that have a habit of either entangling one's feet or catching across the face. But in spite of all drawbacks, some of the party got fairly near the howling dogs, when the baying suddenly ceased and the dogs broke away again on a hot trail, only to tree again within a few hundred yards.

And so it kept up. Whatever it was they were after, it would not stay in a tree for the hunters to come near enough to shine its eyes, and by the time we decided to give up the hunt we were pretty well all in. The experts said it must have been a wild-cat we had been following, and I expect they were right.

By this time we were completely lost, there being no moon or stars to give us a line to get out on, so the good old compass was again called into play.

With it we reached higher ground and built up a fire that would have heated the State Capitol, and for an hour or more we sat on wet logs or leaned against friendly trees in an endeavor to partly dry out and rest up. The compass finally brought us to familiar landmarks, to the boat, and finally to the Club House, which was reached—as before stated—about 3 A. M.

The one man who had been left behind at the house when we started on the hunt had possessed sense enough to have a roaring fire in the big fireplace, so we all went down to the boat house, cut steaks from the carcass of a deer hanging therein, and did quite a job of broiling and eating venison steak before finally turning in for the rest of the night.

You may believe me when I state that that was the roughest coon hunt in which I ever participated.

How heavy was the largest coon you ever saw weighed? The heaviest I ever remember seeing, actual weight, pulled down the scales at fourteen pounds, and the heaviest I know of taken from the afore-mentioned Onslow Club, that was weighed, went eighteen pounds. I was told recently of one taken on the lands of the Tar River and Roanoke Gun Club that weighed twenty-three pounds, and a friend of mine once asserted that years ago he saw a thirty-five pounder! The question still remains, "How big does a coon ever get to be?" And I am not talking about estimates or guesses, but of actual weights on accurate scales. Coons, like fish, surely do shrink in the weighing!

"Minner, How Come!"*

It had taken us some time to make camp and get things in readiness for the tumbling into mosquito-free sleeping quarters at whatever time of night we might want to come off the beach, and this made it late afternoon when we reached the slues on the west side of Brown's Inlet, a locality none of us had ever fished before.

The tide was about half flood and I made my first cast into a likely looking slue near the seaward point of the Inlet. This stage of the tide creates rather peculiar conditions at the sound end of the Inlet. At low water the channel is not more than fifty yards wide, while, as the tide rises, the water quickly covers a flat a hundred yards or more in width flowing over the flat and pouring into a deep hole in the Sound and causing, in connection with the swift current through the channel, a peculiar tide-rip off the Sound Point. And this peculiarity had a bearing on the tragedy.

* Unpublished manuscript.

I soon had a strike—typical channel bass in every particular— and I hooked my fish. He took the line as he wanted it until he reached the strong current in the Inlet channel, and he drove through the Inlet into the frothing waters of the tide-rip previously described. Of course, I followed him along the beach until I was standing on the inner point of the Inlet, with the fish giving me all I wanted and fighting like one of those he-ones that always get away!

And now I had my work cut out. I finally stopped his first long rush, during which I had followed him about three hundred yards, and after sizing up the situation and feeling out the strength of my quarry, I began to work towards getting a little more line back on the reel, on which it now looked mighty slim. I had two hundred yards of new number 15 Joe Jefferson at my disposal so I felt pretty sure of my fish if he proved to be well hooked. However, the quantity of line recoverable was almost negligible for a long time. I would manage to get in ten or fifteen or twenty-five yards and then the fish would step on the gas and I would lose all my gain, and sometimes more. Half an hour went by and my arms and fingers and thumbs were beginning to feel the strain. By that time I figured out that he weighed at least fifty pounds and a little thing like paralyzed muscles did not bother me much.

Another fifteen or twenty minutes passed, with no let up on the part of the fish and no more line on my reel than when he first hit the tide rip. All this time he had fought deep not once showing on the surface, and by the time the hour was up I knew I had a seventy-five pounder at least,—and well hooked at that! Don't think I was doing the timing! I never thought of time in units as small as mere hours, but it turned out that my eldest boy was holding the clock on me, and he called one hour and fifteen minutes when the fight was finally ended.

For more than an hour it had been give and take, with practically nothing gained on either side. My muscles were tiring rapidly, my thumbs and arms were almost paralyzed, but I soon began to realize that the fish was also feeling the effects of the strain, and my reel slowly began to fill up. The only thing that

'aterfowl in flight over vast coastal marshes today represent but a small remnant of rmer millions. (*U. S. Fish and Wildlife Service*)

anada Geese feeding along shore. Coastal North Carolina is one of the principle intering grounds for this fine species. (*N. C. Department of Conservation and De-lopment*)

Raccoon killing a Copperhead Snake.
(*N. C. Department of Conservation and Development*

Fawn of White-tailed Deer comes down to drink.
(*N. C. Department of Conservation and Development*

kept me going was the knowledge that nothing less than a record-breaker plus could put up such a fight as this fish was giving me, and I knew from his methods that he was a channel bass.

But even now he would not give up and every now and then as he came closer, a fierce spurt took back part of the line I had worked so hard to gain. I did not see him until I had him close to the beach,—and then the tragedy! For, in place of the seventy-five pounder plus I had felt certain of, he turned out to be a fish of twenty-eight pounds only!

Had I been familiar then as I am now with the language of the "Military Wildcat" I should have said to my channel bass— "Minner, How Come!"

It was his selection of that tide-rip to fight in that did the trick and wrecked my hopes—and expectations—of the biggest channel bass that ever smashed a line or covered its captor with glory!

Flapper Frolics[*]

T HE FLAPPER is a skeleton-framed, canvas-covered canoe, four-teen feet long by thirty-six inches beam. She is decked fore and aft and has a seven foot cockpit amidships surrounded by a two inch coaming. The fresh, brackish and salt-water reaches of tide-water North Carolina are her stamping ground, and her coaming would be like a fine-tooth saw were it notched for all the fish and game the little ship has brought in.

For a number of years past my wife and I have spent a mid-summer vacation of two or three weeks on, in, and around the broad waters of New River. One morning last August we decided to paddle the Flapper along the river shore—the so-called "river" being about two and a half miles wide at this point—down to Goose Creek, a small tributary of which the fishing qualities seemed to be but little known. "Paddle" is incorrect, however;

[*] Unpublished manuscript.

"shove" would be better, as I kept the boat close to the sandy shore-line and used my long single-blade for poling.

We were silently enjoying the beauties of the early morning, some mullets jumping out in the river having my attention at the time, when Pal, sitting in her canoe chair towards the bow, turned her head slightly and whispered back, "Look, what are those animals?"

I glanced inshore and there, almost abreast of the boat and not more than thirty yards away, were a pair of gray foxes sitting on their haunches on the bare sand and close to the water's edge. My paddle was over the starboard quarter on the offshore side and I pressed the blade down on the hard sand bottom to lessen our headway.

The foxes seemed quite unconcerned, glancing at us or up and down the river without any sign of fear or restlessness. A slight air from the river drifted us slowly in towards them, and I do not think I ever enjoyed a more beautiful and entrancing eye-feast than was presented by that picture in the book of Nature.

The foxes were adults—presumably a pair—and immaculate from nose pad to tail tip. As we drifted to within perhaps twenty-five yards one of them came to a standing position, looked us over rather carefully, then turned tail and gracefully trotted into some scattering dead bushes that fringed a deeper thicket behind. Then it stopped, turned, and looked back.

When the distance between the canoe and the remaining fox had been reduced to about twenty yards, that, too, came to its feet and rejoined its mate, and both silently faded away into the thicket without hurry and without showing anything more than a degree of caution in their movements. And Pal and I agreed that we had been highly favored in being allowed a slight glimpse into the home life of one of the most secretive of the denizens of the wild places.

Goose Creek turned out to be a stinking mudhole, fine for alligators but no good for bass, so we came out on to the river flats, took off shoes and stockings and set about catching a mess of crabs for bait. As soon as we had enough we waded ashore and turned the crabs into bait by removing the shells and cutting up the meat into suitable sized pieces for still-fishing for spotted weakfish, the water being brackish enough even at this distance from the ocean—about a dozen miles—for many species of salt-water fish to frequent.

We had only our five foot casting rods that we had been using for black bass, but we rigged our lines with 2/0 snelled hooks and half ounce sinkers. Paddling out to windward of the "Iron Mine," an area of river bottom rocky in character, we cast our lines out on either side of the canoe and allowed the boat to drift. It was not long before Pal had a strike and hooked some kind of a fighting varmint that tested her tackle to the limit. I soon realized that she was fast to a big gaff-topsail (sea) cat, and I know of no other fish of equal weight that puts up so stubborn a fight. Encouragement was in order, but suddenly I noticed a definite angle between the handle of her rod and the rod itself, and it then dawned on me that water had been in that handle before to the extent of softening the glue. I yelled to her to give him slack and let him shake the hook, or her rod would be a goner. And the hook was shook!

Then, one got mine, and I'm here to say that I was more than tired when I got him into the boat—after hammering his head with the back of my hunting hatchet. This fish turned out to be about the largest sea cat that had ever been caught from the Club. I soon got another—smaller—and then we paddled in, as the gaff-topsails seemed to have taken the Iron Mine for the day, and we had enough.

It was well before sunrise that July morning, in another year, when we started up Cowhead Creek to try for a big 'gator that seemed to have an attraction for a certain section of marsh along the creek bank. As I was to do the shooting, the bow seat in the Flapper was mine for the trip, Pal handling the boat from my usual position in the stern. We both paddled until within two or three hundred yards of our objective, when I shifted paddle for rifle, threw off the safety, and stood by for the next move. Pal is a skilled canoe-handler and the little ship seemed almost to drift of her own accord under the influence of her deft, noiseless strokes.

Slowly the marsh came in sight around a sharp bend, and slowly the canoe glided along, but no sign of 'gator, big or little, greeted our anxious eyes. Without a spoken word, without a sound of any kind, we slowly worked along between the swamp-lined banks until opposite an old log-landing on our left, where the high ground came down to the water's edge and where the bushes had been cleared away for bringing the logs down for rafting. The movement of the boat ceased, and the faintest of whispers came from Pal—"Look!"

I looked, and just back of the landing was a wild turkey hen with young ones. She had seen us—trust a wild turkey for that—and was clucking to her brood as she herded them for cover. But for nearly a minute—or so it seemed—she and several of her chicks were in full sight, a streak of light from the rising sun reflected resplendently from her smooth bronze plumage. And I know of nothing in Nature more beautiful.

"My, but that was worth coming for," said Pal. "We're repaid—and I don't want an old alligator skin traveling bag, anyway. Let's go back to breakfast!" And back to breakfast we went.

At the opposite end of another long summer day we were working down Jumping Run casting for bass as we drifted, with an occasional dip or two of the double paddle to retain our headway and to hold the boat straight. Pal is one of those satisfactory companions who instinctively take in the beauties of these wild swamp streams and who know that gentle movements and absence of noise often afford some opportunity for a little insight into the lives of the wood-folk.

A sudden roar of powerful wings and a crash of branches from a group of trees on the creek bank almost abreast of the canoe—and seven great turkey gobblers left their roosting place and winged their way back into the depths of the swamp. A wild turkey is always grand, but that fact is never impressed on me more strongly than when a big gobbler unexpectedly takes wing from a tree near at hand. Multiply that by seven—and you have a real thrill!

Pal and I were casting for bass up Duck Creek one summer morning when we heard a 'gator bellowing, and the full power of his voice indicated a big bull. I was beginning to despair of ever getting one of these big fellows with my rifle as their shyness and cunning seemed almost uncanny, so this summer I had rigged a couple of lines with the idea of fishing for them. Apart from the use I could make of one or two good hides, I had in mind the fact that we had lost two of our best deer dogs down the throats of these monsters not very long before.

"There's your traveling bag," I remarked to Pal, "let's catch something we can use to bait the hook!" But this turned out to be one of those days when nothing would strike. We worked both sides of the creek for a mile and a half without success, the nearest approach to alligator bait being a jack (pickerel) that struck Pal's bait and only broke loose as I was slipping the landing net under him.

On our way back to the mouth of the creek, where the gas boat was to pick us up about one o'clock, we heard dogs running on the Weil Place. "Suppose we drift along this stretch for a while and see if they put the deer to water," I suggested to Pal. "That suits me, I've never seen a swimming deer and I'd love to!"

But the sound of the dogs began to fade away towards French's Creek, so we started over to the shady side to resume our fishing—when I saw the deer. "Look! There he is. I'll paddle down and give you a sight at short range!"

The deer's head showed small in the water and we soon realized that it was a fawn but, rather stupidly as I thought at the time, it tried to land on the side it had come from. Thinking this poor judgment on the part of the fawn, I headed it off, not wanting to put it ashore on the side the dogs were. They were evidently someone's deer hounds that had got loose but, fortunately, such dogs do little if any harm to the deer in a country intersected by as many broad, twisting creeks as this is.

I got the little fellow turned, and put him ashore on the Foster side of the creek. We had a clear view of his shining, spotted body as he climbed the bank and dashed into the bushes, and you can believe me that he wasted no time in leaving! "That was the most beautiful thing I ever saw in my life," was Pal's comment, and I came pretty near to agreeing with her. Evidently the fawn's mother had given the dogs her scent and had taken them directly away from where she had left her offspring. I feel sure that they got together again that night.

While eating dinner a little later at the Club House we learned that one of a litter of small setter puppies had died during the preceding night—which sounded like alligator bait to me! So, after the meal was over I hunted up the deceased—and that puppy surely was good and dead! He was a fluffy little thing and about the shape of a basket ball when I found him, the weather being hot.

When the sun was getting low that afternoon, I took one of the 'gator lines and fixed the puppy on the hook, tying the body to the leader both back of the fore-legs and forward of the hind-legs, with the hook stuck through the cartilage of one ear. But I would not care for baiting 'gator hooks with ripe puppies as a steady job! In fact, we could not stand it in the boat and had to tow it astern while paddling back to Duck Creek.

Half a mile or so from the mouth of the creek we turned into a twisting gut running back through the marsh from which we had heard the old bull singing earlier in the day. This gut was well known to us as a regular alligator den, and it was here that we had planned to set the baited line. Passing the first bend, I made fast the end of the line to the limber part of a live cedar limb overhanging the water. Then, carrying the line to a dead, partly submerged cedar, I lightly hung the baited hook from the extreme point of one of the snaggy branches, with the bait just above the surface. We backed the canoe a few strokes and looked the outfit over. The setting was perfect—or so it seemed—and as we came into the creek and started back for camp Pal remarked, "I feel sure we will have him in the morning!"

"I think so, too," I replied, "unless some little five or six footer gets to the puppy first, 'cause that's the very choicest thing in baits that was ever placed before an expectant 'gator!"

Early next morning, before the cook had even started a fire, Pal and I were on our way to Duck Creek. All the rest of the bunch in camp were too skeptical to care to go with us—but *we* had expectations! Foolishly, perhaps, I left my rifle at the house and only took along my long-barrelled nine millimeter Luger pistol.

As we entered the gut we could hear the splashing and before we rounded the bend we were fully advised that we had a bite. Tight as a fiddle-string stretched the line from the elastic cedar limb; a few yards farther and the dead cedar came in sight; another stroke—and there came into view the big bull we wanted so much, tearing the water apart in his struggles to get free. One last drive against the straining line, one last lift of his great, rough head, and he went down in a flurry of water that sent the swells surging against the muddy borders of the marsh.

He looked so imposing—in a rough-neck way—that I didn't care to put the frail canoe too close to where he might next rise, so I laid her off a little and stood by with the Luger. Minutes passed, and no sign. More minutes ticked off until half an hour had gone by and still no sign that an alligator had ever been within a mile of the place.

Knowing that no 'gator could remain below for this length of time in water of summer warmth, following the physical exertion this one had just been through, I realized that the mighty effort we had witnessed had resulted in his freedom. But to make sure, we stayed out the hour—and then sadly returned to camp, but only after ascertaining that the 'gator had tied the bight of the line in such a series of turns and twists around the under-water part of the dead cedar limbs as to give him a dead pull against a solid resistance in place of playing on the lively spring of the branch to which the line was attached. And when we took up the line later on we found that the mighty struggles of the big bull had pulled down the hard-twisted wire of the swivel until the eye had been so contracted in diameter as to cut the gang of linen surf lines used as a leader.

One cold winter's day I had been on a deer stand on Cowhead Neck that was most easily reached by taking the canoe to the upper log-landing on Jumping Run. After the unsuccessful hunt was over I was quietly paddling back to camp, with a rather flawy little breeze astern.

When within a hundred or two yards of the main body of French's Creek I noticed a disturbance in the water ahead that I could not at first identify, but it finally dawned on me that it was caused by a pair of otters at play. And that was the winter when fur was at the highest point ever known! And here before me lay an opportunity to secure a valuable piece of fur for Pal that would have a far greater value than its market price by reason of the sentiment attached. So I let the Flapper drift down before the wind, only using the paddle to keep the animals over the port bow.

This was my second experience only of seeing otters undisturbed in their natural surroundings and it was a joy to watch them—and perhaps a sin to attempt to kill! But man is a conglomeration of contradictions and I did not go deeply into the ethics of the situation then.

They were large otters, and the time of the year indicated that their fur was prime. Plunging, rolling and wallowing, they reminded me much of porpoises in some of their stunts—and the canoe continued to drift closer! But the little choppy waves and the flawy breeze made it difficult to hold her in position and lessened her stability as a gun platform. Finally, when both were down at the same time, I laid in my paddle and took up my rifle. Then one appeared, swimming rapidly, with only the top of the head visible. The rifle cracked, and the spout of spray showed that the bullet had gone too high. Then the second otter came up and the bullet intended for him struck short of the mark, and he went down.

That was the last of them, of course, and I haven't seen a live wild otter since.

Digging out a bass was a method Pal and I employed in securing a nice one last summer in Duck Creek. This fish hit my bait pretty near where it fell and before I could stop him he was fast in a tangle of sunken brush and tree-tops near shore, and hung up for keeps. So, while I kept a tight line by taking up the slack, Pal worked the Flapper inshore until the line was up and down. Then I held on to a projecting snag while my partner performed the digging act. But the point where the line was fast was five feet under water and it didn't dig well, so I joined the excavating brigade. Every now and then I managed to get a few inches of line on the reel, but there was no sign of the fish and I was convinced that he had pulled loose. It finally became a question of saving as much line as I could, together with a brand new Shimmy Wiggler with a gorgeous Parmachenee Belle trailer.

It was rather rough digging with a six foot spruce paddle for a spade, the light blade showing a strong tendency to come to the surface, and only one hand being available. Matters were really getting desperate.

"Oh, there he is, close alongside the canoe!" said Pal, as he suddenly appeared among some sunken branches she had stirred up from the coffee-colored depths—and a few moments later he was flopping on the floor-boards between us, a three and a quarter pound big-mouth.

"Well," remarked Pal, with a sigh of relief, "I knew it couldn't be done—but there he is!"

PART THREE

*The Conservation Movement
in North Carolina and Its Region*

EDITOR'S NOTE

In North Carolina, as in other parts of the United States, the first real progress towards conservation of wildlife and other natural resources occurred during the first part of the present century. As indicated in Part I, little or no thought was given to conservation prior to 1900. Of course there had been game laws and local attempts to limit the take of wildlife before this, but it was not until comparatively recently that people in general have become conservation-minded, realizing that what seemed to be an unlimited supply of game was going fast. Also the esthetic value of wild birds and other animals gradually has become recognized so that public opinion for protection of non-game animals has become even stronger than for game in many instances.

Since H. H. Brimley was both sportsman and naturalist it goes without saying that he was also a conservationist. His position as Director of the State Museum gave him the opportunity to sow the seed of conservation in visitors to the museum by means of exhibits. Also, he wrote freely on the subject and, as already indicated, he was a strong backer of T. Gilbert Pearson, a militant worker for conservation.

The first article in this section emphasizes the value of non-game animals and includes an account of the feather trade, a deplorable chapter in our history. The second paper is an excellent historical document, the result of many hours of bibliographical research, which traces man's efforts to conserve wildlife through legislation, not only in North Carolina but in the world.

Bird Conservation in the South°

I HAVE SOMETIMES thought that some of the chief supporters of bird conservation have laid undue stress on the economic value of our birds, with a corresponding lack of importance attached to the esthetic and sentimental side of the subject. Now, I do not in any degree belittle the economic value of our feathered friends, but I do believe that the sentimental and esthetic phase of the subject has at least equal weight with that relating to dollars and cents.

Sitting on my front porch at home, almost any summer evening will show me one or two Acadian Flycatchers using the telephone wire as a lookout. I enjoy their alert attitude, their quick dashes and aerial evolutions after the insect that I cannot see, ending with an audible snap of the bill as the prey is caught. It is the living, pulsing bird that excites my interest—and not the destruction of insect life.

° Condensed from an article originally published in *The Southern Review,* May, 1920.

Then, along towards dusk, more particularly, a pair or two of robins take possession of the lawn. Do I count the number of worms they devour in a given number of minutes and figure therefrom the material benefit the hundred million robins in the United States are to the fruit, grain and vegetable grower? I do not! I watch them and study them as individual living units, apart from me, but perhaps more nearly related to me in some way than I realize.

And the summer tanagers that nest around my home; the brown thrashers, and an occasional wood thrush; all are my friends and all add to the pleasures of living on the edge of the city rather than in an apartment more "convenient" to the tired business man!

The Southern States, as a whole, have been slow in taking a serious and broad-minded view of the problems of game protection and of the conservation of bird-life in general. But in most of them a systematizing and improving of the laws has been carried out in recent years, with a centralized state authority in charge of their enforcement.

Most states, and a majority of the civilized countries of the world, have found that one closed season for the whole state for each individual kind of game is sufficient—and best. In North Carolina we have thirty-six different seasons for deer, and an even forty different seasons for quail! There are nine contiguous counties in the eastern part of the state—in all of which similar conditions prevail—that have fourteen different deer seasons. With such conflicting laws in a comparatively small area, can anyone wonder that they are not observed?

Our laws have been so voluminous, so local in character, and, often, so poorly drawn, that the United States Department of Agriculture has been the only authority that has dared to attempt the publication of a synopsis of them. And last year even the above-named authority gave it up!

Nearly a generation ago, when the great craze for bird plumage for the adornment of women's hats was attaining its growth, the coast line of the Southern States formed breeding grounds for colonies of sea-birds that must, in the aggregate of individuals occupying them, have rivalled in numbers the passenger pigeon when at the height of its abundance.

From the islands north of the Virginia Capes, from Cape Henry to Hatteras, from Hatteras to Key West, up the western coast of Florida and thence to the mouth of the Rio Grande, hundreds, thousands—perhaps tens of thousands—of colonies of gulls and terns increased and multiplied each recurring spring.

But Fashion said that feathers must be worn! And Fashion further decreed that one or two skins of the Least Tern, a single skin of the Forster's Tern or the Common Tern, the wings of a gull or of one of the larger terns, were the really correct thing. Then the slaughter began, spasmodic and amateurish at first, but systematized and business-like later on, until our beaches that had but recently vibrated to the screams of myriads of beautiful wheeling forms lay dead in the June sunshine, with here and there a lonely pair of Wilson's Plover to act as sextons of the teeming graveyards.

Woodland song-birds went, too—warblers, tanagers, orioles, cardinals; anything that wore feathers was worth a price.

Those were pitiful days—but they had their use. A reaction set in. Audubon Societies sprang up all over the country; The National Association of Audubon Societies came into being. And a strong sentiment against the commercialized slaughter of birds was the outcome, with national and state legislation following to give the sentiment practical form.

Here in the South, where we are rather inclined to pride ourselves on our conservatism, practically all of the states now have laws prohibiting the killing of non-game birds at all times, with a few exceptions embracing birds like the crow and the English sparrow of supposedly harmful tendencies. But, in many sections, we are still far short of our duty in the enforcement of our laws.

The egret question has been largely a separate issue. Egret plumes—aigrettes—have always been expensive, and the delicate, lace-like texture of the plume has always appealed to women of refinement and taste. No human artisan has ever produced anything quite so beautiful.

I do not blame the women a bit for the use of these ultra-beautiful sprays for personal adornment—so long as they were ignorant of what their production entailed! But that matter of production is a black, blood-stained chapter in the book of wild-life destruction.

The aigrettes are the nuptial plumes of the parent egrets, worn just before and during the nesting season. The plume-hunters could only work successfully under conditions when the inhabitants of the teeming rookeries were so intent on their individual family interests that they could not be frightened away. And the only time when such conditions prevailed was when there were young, helpless birds in the nests.

A thousand birds in the colony, perhaps; a dozen nests in a tree. Overhead, a few parent birds bringing food to their young.

A shot—and a bird is down; other shots, and more dead egrets on the ground. Still others come in from the sounds and marshes, all intent on the one matter of feeding their young. They are not to be frightened away—and all belonging to that tree are killed.

The plume-hunters move on to another well-occupied tree and the slaughter is repeated until darkness puts an end to the bloody day's work or all the birds with young in their nests have been killed. And the young birds left in the nests? Oh, well! They simply starve to death!

And this is the genesis of the aigrette plume of commerce.

But public sentiment has so strongly condemned this practice that now no aigrettes can be legally taken or sold anywhere in the United States. The egrets, however, have been exterminated in most of their old haunts, and the few remaining colonies are verging on total extinction in the remote fastnesses to which they have been driven. Wardens protecting them have been killed by the outlawed plume-hunters—and the end is not yet! *

"Eagle" quills became fashionable a few years ago, and Brown

---

* Since this article was written twenty-nine years ago, both species of egrets, the American Egret and the Snowy Egret, have made a remarkable recovery and are once again common sights on the waterways of the South.—Editor

Pelicans, Great Blue Herons, and even our Black and Turkey Vultures, were slaughtered to supply the demand.

Perhaps the foregoing embrace the chief and the more conspicuous of the organized attacks upon our bird life, and all of them bore largely on such life in the Southern States. These conditions, together with the known decrease in our game, have added many laws to our statute books, many good ones, some positively bad, and a few ridiculous. Many people still believe, however, that the mere adoption of a law automatically remedies the condition that called it into being. Such people I should class as ingrowing optimists. But I qualify the above remarks by stating that the moral effect of the adoption of a law is sometimes as effective as its physical enforcement.

Some fishermen yet take eggs of the Royal Tern for food, and the boy with his first gun has still the desire to shoot anything that moves or flies. But neither practice is as prevalent as it was half a generation ago. Public sentiment is often slow to crystallize, and it has been slow with us in its relation to bird protection.

We now come to a group of birds that has been woefully misunderstood in the past. I am referring to the predacious species—the hawks and owls. To most people a hawk is a hawk —just as a snake is a snake—to be killed on sight. At times, official bounties have been offered for hawk scalps, but we are learning more of the habits and the food of our birds all the time and beginning to understand some of them better than our fathers did—and bounties are no longer popular.

Many of our owls and hawks are not only harmless in their relation to other birds and to humanity but are positively beneficial. The Barn and the Barred Owls, the Short-eared and Long-eared Owls, and the Screech Owl, are all beneficial species. The Red-tailed, Red-shouldered and Broad-winged Hawks, the Marsh Hawk and the Sparrow Hawk, are all much more beneficial than harmful, some of them feeding almost exclusively on field rats and mice. Others—the Sparrow Hawk, for instance—seem to prefer an insect diet. All of the above-named hawks and owls should be protected, but the practical side of their protection is a difficult problem for the reason that most people are not competent to distinguish the species, and therefore make a practice of shooting every hawk and owl on sight—as an actual or prospective chicken-eater.

There are a few species, however, for which we cannot find much economic reason for protecting. This group contains the Great Horned Owl, the Cooper's Hawk and the Sharp-shinned Hawk. The first of the three is perhaps the most destructive bird of prey found in America. Certain it is that in the Southern States the Great Horned Owl and the Cooper's Hawk are responsible for more casualties among the farmers' poultry and among our game birds than all other birds of prey combined. But, personally, I cannot but admire a Great Horned Owl for his strength and courage, and the aggressive fearlessness of the Cooper's Hawk when in pursuit of prey also excites my admiration. But, then, I do not live in the country—or keep chickens!

The Sharp-shinned Hawk is the most consistent bird-destroyer of the lot, its food being birds almost exclusively. It is too small a hawk, however, to be very destructive to poultry and game birds.

The two last species mentioned are the ones often heard referred to as Blue Darters, or Blue-tailed Darters.

For those engaged in game farming it will often be found necessary to protect the young stock from the depredations of their natural, ground-living enemies, including mink, weasel, fox, coon, possum, and, sometimes, wildcat. Under natural conditions, however, it is doubtful policy to interfere with the balance of Nature by any particular efforts to exterminate the four-footed enemies of birds. Nature can usually be depended on to make her balance swing true.

In a final reference to the condition of bird and game protection in the Southern States, I would say that what we need to carry on the good work that has been so well started in many of them is a campaign of popular education in the matter.

Many men of more than average intelligence—good, law-abiding citizens at home—seem to have the idea when they reach their favorite deer, or turkey or duck-shooting grounds that all game laws are for the other fellow! Any bird or animal that flies, swims or walks is a fair target for their ever-ready guns, and a grebe gets killed for a duck, a deer is shot in the water, and a hovering gull falls a victim just because it possesses organs of flight. A woodpecker climbing a tree trunk is such a good target for a .22 rifle, a robin eating cedar berries is shot just to see it fall (the robin was "game" with us until quite recently), and a cormorant on a stake receives a load of shot for the pleasure of seeing it fly!

A Sketch of the History of Wildlife Conservation in North Carolina*

B<small>EFORE</small> <small>ENTERING</small> into the history of the conservation of wildlife in North Carolina, it would seem appropriate to present a brief sketch of what had previously been done in earlier days by other peoples as a background to what follows.

The first conservation law of which I have knowledge is to be found in the Bible, Deuteronomy, Chapter XXII, Verses 6 and 7, where it is provided that the young or eggs of a bird may be taken from the nest, but the female bird must be spared.

Previous to the Conquest of England by the Normans in A. D. 1066, there was a law that prohibited hunting on Sundays, perhaps the first real game law. Later, monks were forbidden to hunt in the wood with dogs. And, when notice was given that the King would hunt on a certain day, no one else in that imme-

* From Bulletin No. 1 of Division of Game and Inland Fisheries, North Carolina Department of Conservation and Development, Raleigh, N. C., 1939.

diate territory, noble or otherwise, was allowed to take the field. Following the Conquest, hunting was restricted to the nobility and heavy penalties were imposed on those who failed to abide by the stringent game laws that had been enacted; hence, the banding together of outlaws of the Robin Hood type whose love of the chase could not be squelched by any kind of a game law, so they used their bows and arrows on the red deer even at the risk of the hangman's noose.

"The Master of Game," a book on hunting written by Edward, Duke of York, about 1412, and reprinted in 1909, is probably the oldest book on this subject. I was rather surprised to find in it the following statement: "But as for hunting (as compared with hawking) there is no season of all the year that game may not be found in every good country, also hounds ready to chase it. And since this book shall be all of hunting, which is so noble a game, and lasting through all the year of divers beasts that grow according to the season for the gladdening of man, I think I may well call it Master of Game."

However, later in the book one discovers that a "fence-month" was in force that forbade not only the hunting of deer during the month that ran from 15 days before to 15 days after, midsummer, but also any disturbance of the animals during that period even to the extent of keeping all swine, cattle and stray dogs out of the woods, with watch and ward kept by men with weapons. These protectors may have been the first game wardens on record.

In Izaac Walton's "Compleat Angler," published in 1653, the author mentions certain "fence-months," in which fish might not be taken, March, April and May being mentioned, particularly, to cover the spawning season of the salmon. Walton also calls attention to "wise statutes" made during the reigns of King Edward I (1272-1307) and King Richard III (1483-1485) in which "one may find several provisions made against the destruction of fish."

From "The Gentleman's Recreation, a Treatise of Hawking and Faulconry," published in 1674, I am quoting the following extracts:

From "An Abstract of such Statute Laws as concern Fowling":

"None shall destroy or take away the Eggs of any Wild-fowl, in pain to forfeit for every Egg *or* a Crane or Bustard so taken or destroyed twenty pence. Of a Bittern, Hern (heron) or Shoveland eight pence. And of a Mallard, Teal or other Wild-fowl one penny, to be divided between the King and the Prosecutor."

"None shall hawk or hunt with his Spaniels in standing grain, or before it is shocked (except in his own Ground, or with the Owner's consent) in pain to forfeit forty shillings to the Owner of the said Ground."

"Every Constable or Headborough (upon warrant under the hand of two Justices of the Peace) hath power to search the Houses of persons suspected to have any Setting Dogs or Nets for the taking of Pheasants or Partridges; and the Dogs or Nets there found to kill and cut to pieces at pleasure, as things forfeited unto the said Officers."

The abstracts also include laws against the following practices: Hunting on another's land without permission, the sale of game that is not hand-reared, night hunting, and the taking of Pheasant or Partridge between the first of July and the last of August.

These laws, made more than 300 years ago, contain principles that are still recognized by conservationists, such as the non-destruction of property when hunting on another's land, the preservation of the nests of game birds, the non-sale of game, the requirement of permission to hunt on another's land, the prohibition of hunting at night, and closed seasons for game. So, the official control and conservation of wildlife is not as modern a problem as some of us have been inclined to believe.

In 1936, the Luton Museum, of Luton, Bedfordshire, England, published a most interesting volume entitled "Bedfordshire Vermin Payments," in which are listed a vast number of items relating to bounties paid for the destruction of vermin in the various parishes into which the county is divided, the entries dating from 1563 to 1872. The data is mainly made up of extracts from church records, the church wardens in those days being the administrative officers of the individual parishes.

People in general, even parish officials, were not exactly literate in the earlier days of these payments and the spellings are, in places, something wonderful and fearful to behold. The word "fox" is spelled in 9 different ways; "mole," 14; and "otter," 19. In 177 entries for weasel, there are 32 variations in spelling; 53 for polecat; and no less than 80 for hedge-hog.

It would seem that the fund for the paying of bounties must have been rather elastic in its application, judging from the following extracts:

"1687. Item paid to Robert Clarke for Clarkes Sheep (clerkship) and mole cating and for washing of the surplish (surplice) and other table linen for the Comemuneion table this yeare last part, £2.1s.0d."

"1808. Bout a drink for Jona Rowletts Daughter Bit by a Mad Dog, 5s." "Cleaning the church of Dogs, 4s."

As most of the foregoing matter relates to how the game situation was handled in England in the early days, we may now pass on to a sketch of its history in the United States.

The protection of the game itself, rather than the grant of exclusive game rights to certain exalted personages, has, from the first, been the principle on which the game laws of the United States have been based. The earliest U. S. game law of which I can find a record was when in 1623, the Plymouth Colony declared hunting, fishing and fowling to be free, except on certain private property, but that wild game and fish were not to be molested during their reproduction seasons.

However, as the pioneers began their movements to the south and west from the first settlements on the east coast, wild game was their main sustenance and for a long period necessity called for the killing of such game as was needed pretty much irrespective of the time of year. Such killing, however, had little effect in reducing the supply.

Deer, bear, turkey, passenger pigeons and wildfowl were found in such abundance as to make it certain to the pioneer hunters that these vast resources of food supply could never be exhausted, and real conservation laws were so slow in coming that much of our game had been reduced to the point of exhaustion before definite and drastic laws were enacted for the preservation of the pitiful remnants.

Not that anyone is particularly to blame for this. No one could foresee how rapidly the game would disappear. The bison (American buffalo) had to give way to the farmer and the cattleman on the western plains and there is no need to shed tears over what occurred. It was an economic question that had to be answered in favor of the agriculturist. But there are many more thousands of bison today in the country than there were 20 or 30 years ago.

The passenger pigeon might, perhaps, have been retained as a fairly common species had the country become conservation-conscious earlier than it did. Everyone conversant with the bird realized that it was decreasing in numbers but it became extinct before anyone realized that it was nearing the danger point, and there was no come-back in this case.

States' Rights was the rallying cry and the oversight of the game and other natural resources of the country was left in the hands of the individual states, with disastrous results.

When we come to the history of wildlife conservation in North Carolina, we are confronted with the problem of knowing where to start. Up to fairly recent times, our people had been so used to the belief in local self-government, with the preservation of our game a matter to be handled individually by each of our large number of counties, that State-wide laws on the subject had been very few in number.

PROTECTION OF DEER RECOGNIZED BY LAW IN 1745

Some difficulty was found in trying to trace back the earlier laws of the State as they relate to game considered as a State-wide problem, but one was finally dug up that would appear to be worth presenting in full as, besides calling attention to the fact the deer appeared to be the only species of game deserving of protection, it also provides an insight into the long hunting season allowed (seven months) as well as the tendency of irresponsible persons to ignore any law restricting what they considered their inherited privileges. This law, enacted by the General Assembly of the Province of North Carolina in 1745, is given in Chapter III, Laws of 1745, as follows:

"An additional Act to an Act, to prevent killing Deer at unseasonable Time, and for putting a Stop to many Abuses committed by white Persons, under Pretense of hunting.

"I. Whereas by the before-recited Act, it is, among other Things, Enacted, That it shall not be lawful for any Person to kill or destroy any Deer, running wild in the Woods or unfenced Grounds in this Government, by Guns, or any other Ways or Means whatsoever, between the Fifteenth Day of February and the Fifteenth Day of July, Yearly, and in each Year, after the Ratification of the said Act; and that any Person convicted of the same, shall forfeit and pay the Summ of Five Pounds, current Money: and whereas it appears, that the allowing Liberty of killing Deer in fences Grounds and Inclosures at such Seasons, has given Room to several Persons to evade the said Law:

"II. We therefore pray that it may be Enacted, and be it Enacted, by his Excellency Gabriel Johnston, Esq., Governor, by and with the Advice and Consent of his Majesty's Council, and General Assembly of this Province, and it is hereby Enacted, by the authority of the same, That if any Person shall be convicted of killing Deer, or having Venison, or a green Deer skin, or Skins, in his House, Camp, or Possession, between the Fifteenth Day of February, and the Fifteenth Day of July, Yearly, after the Ratification of this Act, he shall forfeit and pay the Summ of Forty Shillings, Proclamation Money; to be recovered and applied as herein after directed.

"III. Provided nevertheless, That nothing in this Act shall be construed to extend or convict any Person or Persons of the said Forfeiture, in whose House any Venison, green Skin or Skins, shall be found, which hath been left in such House without the Knowledge, Privity or Consent of such Person, or any of his family, upon due proof thereof to be made, by the Person therewith charged.

"IV. And forasmuch as there are great Numbers of idle or disorderly Persons, who have no settled Habitation, nor visible

Method of supporting themselves, by Industry or honest Calling, many of whom come in from neighboring Colonies, without proper Passes, and kill Deer at all Seasons of the Year, and often leave the Carcasses in the Woods, and also steal and destroy Cattle, and carry away Horses, and commit other Enormities, to the great Prejudice of the Inhabitants of this Province; be it therefore Enacted, by the Authority aforesaid, That every person who shall hunt and kill Deer in the King's Wast within this Province, and who is not possessed of a settled Habitation in the same, shall be obliged to produce a Certificate, when required, of his having planted and tended Five Thousand Corn hills, at Five Feet Distance each Hill, the preceding Year, or Season, in the County where he shall hunt, under the Hands of at least Two Justices of the Peace in said County, and the Hand of at least one of the Churchwardens of the Parish where such Person planted and tended such Corn, as aforesaid.

"V. And be it further enacted, That if any such Person as aforesaid is found hunting and does not produce such Certificate, when required, he shall forfeit his Gun and Five Pounds, Proclamation Money, for every such Offense; to be recovered and applied as herein after directed.

"VI. And whereas many idle Persons, who spend their chief Time in hunting Deer, leave the Carcasses in the Woods, by which means Wolves, Bears and other Vermin are raised and supported, which destroy the Stocks of the Inhabitants of this Province; be it therefore Enacted by the Authority aforesaid, That every Person who hunts Deer, and leaves the Carcass or Carcasses in the Woods, undestroyed, shall for every Offence, forfeit and pay Forty Shillings, Proclamation Money.

"VII. And be it further Enacted, by the Authority aforesaid, That all fines and Forfeitures mentioned in this Act, shall be paid, the One Half to the Informer, the other Half to the Church wardens, for the use of the Parish wherein such offense shall be committed, to be recovered, with Costs, by a warrant from any Justice of the Peace within this Government; saving to all free Persons the Right of Appeal to the County Court where such Offense is committed: Which Court is hereby impowered and directed, in a summary Way, finally to determine the same; wherein no Essoign, Protection, or Wager of Law, shall be allowed or admitted of."

In the Code of 1854, I could find nothing in the index under Quail, Game, County Game, or Local Game statutes. When I tried "Deer," I found a reference to "Burning Woods," and under that title was found a law to the effect that 2 days before burning off woods notice must be given to all adjoining property owners, with a maximum penalty of $50 provided for infraction. Directly following this the closed season for deer was given as February 20 to August 15, allowing an open season of six months.

LAWS PROVIDING FOR PROTECTION OF OTHER WILDLIFE

In the Code of 1883, the following State laws relating to game were found: Hunting deer by firelighting was forbidden, with references to laws of 1784, 1801, 1856-57 and 1879. The deer season was August 15 to February 15. In 1868, firelighting of wild-fowl was prohibited. In 1870-71, it was made illegal to shoot wild-fowl at night or on Sunday, or by a gun that could not be fired from the shoulder. In 1874 and 1881, the taking of partridge, quail, dove, robin, lark, mockingbird or wild turkey was illegal from April 1 to October 15. Five and a half months allowed for the shooting of robins, larks and mockingbirds! There seemed to be no protection of any kind for any other form of wildlife than the four game birds and three non-game species protected by the act.

Prohibition of shipping quail out of the State became a law in 1876, and the open season for wildfowl in Currituck County was made November 10 to March 10, with no shipments during the closed season. Non-residents (of the State, I presume) were prohibited from using a battery or other floating device for wild-fowl shooting in Currituck and Dare Counties.

And so we dragged along, the spirit of conservation not being in us. In fact, the phrase "Conservation of Natural Resources" was unknown to us and we blindly went ahead passing many additional county game laws at every session of the Legislature.

So many people thought—and often still think it—that all we have to do to relieve a situation is to Pass a Law. As a matter of fact, passing a law is often equivalent to passing the buck!

LOCAL GAME LAWS MANY AND DIVERSE

But we surely did not fail to pass local game laws, the following figures being taken from publications of the Bureau of Biological Survey of the United States Department of Agriculture: In 1909, 43 states in which the Legislatures had been in session passed 215 laws relating to game—and North Carolina was responsible for 79 of them! In 1911, the 43 states adopted game laws to the number of 260, of which 71 were passed by the Legislature of this State. In 1915, North Carolina put 61 new laws relating to game on the Statute books, out of 240 by the 43 states as a whole. Can you beat that! Judging from these figures, it would be reasonable to believe that in the earlier days of this century we had on our Statute books from one-fourth to one-fifth of all the game laws of all the states in the Union with, perhaps, as low a rate of enforcement as any.

I do not mean to infer that none of the legislation of this period was constructive. A very small proportion of the laws were State-wide in character, prohibiting the shipping of live quail out of the State for stocking purposes being one of them, but it is the general attitude of the Legislature, representing the opinions of our citizenship at large, to which attention is directed.

STATE-CONTROL OF WILDLIFE RECOGNIZED

It was not until 1903 that T. Gilbert Pearson, teacher of Biology at the North Carolina College for Women, in Greensboro, came to the rescue. After heroic efforts, he succeeded in securing the passage of an Act of the Legislature that provided for the protection of song-birds and placed the administration of this phase of the new law, and the administration of the local game laws then on the Statute books, under the North Carolina Audubon Society, of which Pearson was the executive officer.

This was the first step towards recognizing the principle of State control of our wildlife.

Previous to this, the administration of the vast number of county and other local game laws lay with the county officials. Becoming interested in the matter at that time, I had occasion to make some study of these local laws. I found that the various counties had more than forty different hunting seasons for Bob-White and about the same number for deer. I also found that nine adjoining counties in the eastern part of the State, in which almost exactly the same physical conditions prevailed, had no less than 13 different deer seasons, some of them applying only to a single township. In one eastern county, deer were given no protection, it being perfectly legal to kill a deer while nursing her fawns—and then kill the fawns! In another county, the deer season opened on the fourth of July, the summer killing of deer for fresh meat being quite generally practiced. Quail netting was not frowned upon in many of the best quail counties, bullbats were shot just to see them fall and robins were quite generally killed for food purposes.

Along our coast-line, gulls, terns and egrets were slaughtered by the hundreds of thousands for the millinery trade and, on the sounds up and down the coast, wildfowl were killed for the market in very large numbers but no definite figures are available, all this being done legally, with no bag-limit on anything and not much practical restriction as to open seasons in the case of any of our game.

"How are we goin' to git fresh meat in summer if we kaint go out and kill us a deer," or "There allus has been plenty of chub in the crick and we aim to keep on ketchin' 'em when we damn please," represent the attitude taken by many of the old time hunters and fishermen of those days.

One should go slow, however, in too severely condemning these old believers in a Divine right to take fish and game at any time in any numbers in the days before the principles of conservation began to be accepted and the knowledge of them diffused. They had been brought up in the belief that the wild creatures of the woods and waters had been placed there specifically for the use of those humans fortunate enough to live in contact with the birds and animals, and they strongly resented any attempt to curtail such privileges. As an instance of how such ideas have been retained in isolated localities even up to recent days, I may say that a United States under-cover man told me two or three years ago of an investigation trip he had recently made to a certain island in one of the large bodies of water bordering the Atlantic coast of the United States that had become notorious as being the supposed center for a group of market hunters who were taking great numbers of ducks illegally and disposing of them through the game bootleggers.

He visited the island in the character of a collector of speci-mens of birds for a museum. The island's inhabitants proved to be a closely knit and closely related body of individuals, deeply religious in character, and thoroughly saturated with a belief in their Divine right to slaughter ducks by any means and in any numbers and to sell them on an illegal market. They were taking ducks both by fire-lighting with huge swivel guns and also by trapping them alive on the marshes. The investigator must have excited some shadow of suspicion for, in spite of the very precise and primitive rules of religion under which the islanders lived, he was casually given to understand that any stranger visiting the island with the idea of getting them into trouble would be taken out on the bay some dark night and dropped overboard in deep water with a heavy anchor made fast to his neck!

T. GILBERT PEARSON AND THE "AUDUBON LAW"

But to go back to the adoption of the so-called "Audubon Law" in 1903.

When Pearson, as executive officer of the State Audubon So-ciety, took over the administration of the new law protecting song-birds and the conflicting mass of local game laws in force in the 97 counties of the State, he was faced with a very difficult situation, or perhaps it would be better to say, quite a number of difficult situations.

The robin had always been considered a game and food bird in the rural districts, and robin-pie was by no means unknown to the dwellers of our cities, but now this succulent dish was prohibited. No longer could the swirling bullbat be legally used as a flying target for our gunners, and we could not legally take the young mockingbirds for cage pets. From the boy with the Flobert rifle had been taken the joy of shooting song-birds in the shade-trees around the house, and the dweller in the country who was accustomed to go out and kill a mess of squirrels or quail for the family table at any time of the year he saw fit was now to learn of the existence of a new kind of official known as a Game Warden. Then, too, if the wardens were local men, working on small salaries, they were naturally loath to arrest men of prominence in their communities who were found committing infractions of the new laws. The apathy of the general public on this matter of game and bird protection was another obstacle in the path.

The limited funds available for the administration of the law was a further serious handicap, the only money made available by the Act being that resulting from a ten dollar license fee to be collected from each non-resident hunter. It was no bed of roses into which T. Gilbert Pearson had fallen. But Pearson was an educator, a pioneer, an enthusiast (I might almost say a Moses) with a mission, and the most compelling public-speaker —particularly on the subject of bird-protection—I have ever known. A fine organizer and administrator and, coming from good old Quaker stock, the word "failure" was not in his vocabulary. So he plunged ahead.

Quite naturally, he got into deep water, but, by organizing local Audubon Societies all over the State, by preaching bird protection at every available opportunity, he so far educated the coming generation to the point where many of our people were slowly becoming conservation-conscious.

It is not necessary to go into the details of the difficulties encountered by Pearson in his efforts for the protection of our birds. Needless to say, he did a noble work—but made a lot of enemies in his efforts to carry out the new law. As Legislature succeeded

Legislature, county after county had its name stricken from the list of those under the administration of the Audubon Society, until, in 1910, Pearson was called to a larger field of work as Secretary and executive officer of the National Association of Audubon Societies, with headquarters in New York, of which he had been Secretary, under President William Dutcher, since 1905.

In the years immediately following Pearson's acceptance of a much wider scope of work in another state, no enthusiastic conservationist was found to take his place. Sympathizers with his efforts were many but all such were men engaged in making a living in other lines with but little time to devote to the matter in which Pearson had been the leader and controlling spirit.

Another reason for the increase in opposition to the so-called "Audubon Law" was the realization that a peculiar condition had been created, that the administration of a certain group of laws, the collection of privilege taxes connected therewith (non-resident license fees), and the disbursement of State funds had been placed in the hands of a self-perpetuating corporation.

The drift of counties away from the control of the Audubon Society increased until its income had dwindled to the point where no progressive or constructive work was longer possible. So, the Directors of the Society decided to approach the Legislature with a real State-wide game bill, including the establishment of a State Game Commission.

STATE-WIDE GAME BILL DRAFTED

With all the information available in other States in which this method of game conservation had proved successful, and with a knowledge of conditions in North Carolina, a bill was drafted and submitted to the Legislature of 1913. This was the first attempt to place our game birds and animals under State-wide control with uniform open seasons. Circulars showing the need for a change in game law administration in North Carolina, signed by the late Dr. R. H. Lewis, President of the Audubon Society, and by the writer, as Vice-President, were prepared and distributed, and both of us appeared before the Game Committees of the Legislature in support of the bill.

As expected, the bill failed to pass; in fact, it was given very little serious consideration except by its sponsors. But the entering wedge had been driven in.

In 1915, 1917, 1919, and 1921, the Audubon Society introduced other bills along the same lines, each one an improvement and modernization of its predecessor. Each was killed in its turn, but public sentiment was slowly taking form and the opponents of the plan gradually discovered that these bills required more and more effort to bring about their defeat.

In 1923, Representative Wade, of New Hanover County, introduced a bill, based on the previous Audubon Society's bills, which was also defeated.

In 1925, two bills were introduced, the Wade-Graham Bill and the N. C. Fish and Game League Bill, the main features of each being those of the bills submitted in previous years by the Audubon Society.

But public sentiment, after having undergone a process of evolution along with the character of the bills, had by then crystallized to the point where the opponents of the measure had to use their utmost efforts to prevent the substitute for the two original bills becoming a law.

The 1927 bill, which in amended form became the law of the State, as it related to game, was a further development of the bills that had preceded it, though again modified to suit new developments and changing conditions. This bill was introduced by Mr. Fred Sutton, of Kinston, who ably piloted it to its final success. This was the first Act to abolish the mass of local game laws that had proved so unsatisfactory, the first recognition of the principle of State-wide seasons for game, and it contained the first provision for licensing the resident hunter and fisherman, previous game licenses being imposed only on non-resident hunters. In other words, we had at last emerged from the woods.

It will be seen from the foregoing that the present legal status of the control of game in North Carolina is the direct result of efforts that began a number of years earlier. And all this is largely preliminary to one of the main points that I want particularly to stress.

This point is the fact that the long, worrying, and sometimes seemingly hopeless efforts towards the ends sought had all been accompanied by a slow-moving but steadily-growing public sentiment in favor of taking the only action possible to properly protect, preserve and rehabilitate our game, and other forms of wildlife.

It will not do to omit one important factor that has done more to protect our wildfowl, shore birds and other migratory species, than any local legislation could have done, this being the Migratory Bird Treaty between the United States and Canada in 1913, followed by the Enabling Act adopted by Congress in 1918. The North Carolina Legislature of 1931 enacted an amendment to our State-wide game law making it conform to the Federal Enabling Act and the regulations adopted by the United States Department of Agriculture under the said act.

But—and this word must be in capitals—the cooperation of the public is essential in the carrying out of any phase of conservation work. This means that all hunters and all fishermen, together with every one in any way interested in the conservation of our wild birds, wild animals and our forests, must not only do their best to abide by the laws and regulations, but must also actively cooperate with the Conservation officers in their efforts to administer these regulations. It is so much easier to quench a camp-fire, or grind a burning cigarette stump into the moist ground, than it is to fight a forest fire! And think of the other fellow and the younger generation coming into its own when the fish are striking and you are tempted to exceed your legal limit. This mean YOU and this means ME!

PART FOUR

The Giants of Nature: Whales and Other Large Animals

EDITOR'S NOTE

When it comes to size in the animal kingdom, many people think of the great prehistoric dinosaurs, the sixty-foot Brontosaurus in particular, as being the largest known animals. However, several of our modern whales exceed both in length and bulk the greatest of the extinct reptiles and are actually the largest animals ever known, past or present. H. H. Brimley held a lifelong interest in whales, perhaps because his first job with the State Museum was the preparation of a whale skeleton or perhaps because it is only natural to expect that a naturalist possessed with such a buoyant, expansive personality as he would be interested in these great aquatic mammals. As a result of his interest, the North Carolina State Museum has probably the finest collection of whale exhibits of any museum of its size. Other great denizens of land and sea, especially the sharks, the ocean sunfish (Mola mola), the devilfish (Manta birostris), and the great extinct mammoths and mastodons were also among his favorite topics for study and for articles and talks. Since his technical papers are already well known to specialists in the field, I have selected four manuscripts, largely heretofore unpublished, which will be of greater interest to the general reader. These articles show a good synthesis of factual background material and personal, "human interest" experiences interestingly told.

Whales[*]

THE WHALES constitute a group of carnivorous mammals whose structure and mode of life have been modified to suit their aquatic habits. Beginning with the size of these interesting creatures, we find a great variation in the different species—which number about eighty in all—the great Blue Whale reaching a length of one hundred feet and the little Pontoporia Porpoise of the Amazon River not exceeding four feet in length.

Old writers, however, were not content with even such measurements as the maximum given above. Pliny speaks of fish in the India Sea as being "so long and broad as to take up more length and breadth than two acres of ground," which would indicate a whale about 840 feet long by 105 feet broad! He also mentions a length of 900 feet. Claus Magnus gives a length of 960 feet to certain "hirsute" whales. And the latter author has this further to say of the Sperm Whale: "The Physeter raises itself above the

* Unpublished manuscript written about 1940, although some of the material was used in various newspaper articles.

masts of ships and belches forth draughts of ocean from its blow-holes in such a way that it overwhelms with this rainy cloud even the strongest ships, or exposes the sailors to the greatest danger." This latter statement is based on the fact that when a large whale exhales, the moisture-laden breath is often condensed to a foggy plume, as is the breath of humans on a frosty morning. This plume—or "spout," as the whalers call it —would not exceed 12 or 15 feet in height in the case of even a large Sperm Whale. And it would consist of foggy matter, not "draughts of ocean"!

There was plenty of this exaggerated form of writing on the subject by the earlier contributors to knowledge, but the foregoing should be sufficient to show that those old boys did not lack imagination.

The external shape of all members of the order is quite uniform, there being no such divergence in either outline or proportion as we find among land animals, or among such forms of fish as live very much the same kind of life as do the whales. It should be remembered, however, that the caudal fin—or "flukes," as the whalers call it—is placed in a horizontal plane and not vertical as is the case with fishes.

Such marked differences in form as occur among this group are largely confined to the head and to the depth of the body compared with its total length. The tail is of the same general shape in all species. The flippers (pectoral fins) vary from rounded to pointed at the tips, the maximum variation in length being found in the Humpback Whale whose extremely long flippers may measure as much as a third of the length of the body. The pelvis is represented by one or two small floating bones situated where a pelvis might be expected.

Generally speaking, the whales are marine in their habits, the few exceptions belonging to the group that includes the porpoises and dolphins, some of which inhabit such rivers as the Amazon, the Ganges, the Yangtse, etc., spending their lives in fresh water.

Whales, as a whole, show no external indications of a neck as in most species the cervical vertebrae are fused together, the neck being shorter in proportion than in any other group of mammals. The Narwhal and the White Whale, however, do have a trifle of play to the neck, the vertebrae in their cases being free, and not fused. Not much opportunity for any rubber-neck business for these short-necked whale creatures!

Whales are divided into two main groups, the Mysticeti, or Whalebone Whales, and the Odontoceti, or Toothed Whales. A peculiarity of the latter group is the asymmetry of the skull in all the species, a character not found in any other group of vertebrate animals. This feature reaches its maximum, perhaps in the great Sperm Whale, in which the nasal passage in running up from the throat, makes a turn to the left and follows the left side of the long head to the tip of the great truncated snout, where it ends in an S-shaped blowhole which is situated on the left of the center line of the head. Something like having one's nose growing out of one's cheek instead of the center of the face. Which, in humans, might well prevent even a female face from reaching the acme of pulchritude! This asymmetrical feature is quite noticeable in the skulls of all members of the group.

Up to comparatively recent years, only about three species of whale had been systematically hunted commercially. The most valuable of all in the old days of the "fishery" was the Bowhead, or Greenland Whale, which occurs only in the Arctic seas. This great creature, the most bulky of all whales for its length, and living in the icy waters of the Arctic, naturally carried an exceptionally thick coating of blubber, which meant, of course, a maximum production of oil per specimen. But its greatest value lay in the whalebone (baleen), which in a large animal might run ten or eleven feet in length and yield, perhaps, a total weight of 3,000 pounds, or more. And the crude "bone" sold for several dollars a pound. So, in the Good Old Days, a large Bowhead would be worth ten or twelve thousand dollars to its captors and, occasionally, even more than that. Captain Scammon,* an authority on the subject, gives the maximum yield of oil

* C. H. Scammon, *The Marine Mammals of the Northwest Coast of North America, Together with an Account of the American Whale Fishery* (G. P. Putnam's Sons, 1874).

for this species as 275 barrels or 13,750 gallons, and the maximum weight of whalebone as 3,500 pounds.

Second in value was, probably, the Sperm Whale, the largest of the whales that have teeth. This species has no whalebone and has teeth in the lower jaw only. The sperm oil tried out from its blubber was more valuable than common "whale oil" and, in addition, the liquid wax, known as spermaceti, secreted in a huge tank, situated on the right-hand side of the head, formed a large additional source of revenue. Ten to fifteen barrels, or more, of this valuable substance might be dipped from the "old head" of a large Sperm Whale. About sixty feet seems to be the maximum length of this species.

The last of the three most valuable whales was the Right Whale, a smaller edition of the Bowhead, found in the more temperate seas and in nearly all the oceans. It is somewhat more refined in its proportions than the Bowhead, if one may use such a word in connection with an animal more than fifty feet in length and fourteen or fifteen feet in depth of body! The blubber of the Right Whale averages less in thickness than that of the Bowhead and therefore produces a smaller quantity of oil, though Scammon mentions more than 200 barrels taken from a single specimen.

The old whaling days have gone forever. The expensive whale-bone has been superseded by much cheaper and equally efficient non-corrodible elastic substances, and various derivatives of petroleum have largely replaced the whale oils. Further, the two species of whalebone whales mainly sought by the old-time whale ships have decreased in number to such an extent that their pursuit is no longer a profitable venture.

Not that whaling is extinct, by any means, but the methods of taking whales have changed, and the species now sought are those that were passed up as valueless by the old timers.

For many years there was very little material change in the methods employed in taking whales. The whale-boat, propelled by sail and oars, and manned by a crew of six men—boat-steerer, boat-header and four seamen at the oars—was run up on the whale's back, or as close as possible, and the harpoon thrown into the animal's body. The whale promptly sounded, the boat backed off, the line attached to the harpoon—which was coiled in a tub and about 400 fathoms in length—ran out, and the boat followed the direction of the line so as to be as close up as possible when the whale next rose to breathe. One or two extra 400-fathom tubs of line were usually carried as a reserve, to be attached to the harpoon line in case all of the first tub should be taken out by the whale.

WHALE BOAT & CREW

Then the boat-header, who had changed places with the boat-steerer, or harpooner, handled the long lance with which the animal was finally killed by repeated thrusts into the lungs.

More than fifty years ago, the place of the lance for killing purposes was partly taken over by a bomb-gun attached to the shank of the harpoon, which automatically fired a small bomb into the whale's body after the harpoon had been driven in. This was later supplemented by an independent bomb-gun fired from the shoulder of the boat-header.

This gun was all iron, including the stock, a loop being forged on the latter. To this loop a line was spliced, the other end of the line being made fast in the boat so that if both man and gun were kicked overboard by the recoil, the gun would be saved! Incidentally, the man would also be picked up.

The culmination of the old-style method of whaling was around the year 1846, when 730 American ships were engaged in the industry, Americans completely dominating the business at that time. The industry is now centered in the Antarctic and has, up to quite recently, virtually been controlled by the Norwegians.

The modern method of taking whales is from shore stations or floating factories. The actual killing is done by means of heavy harpoons fired from small cannon mounted in the bows of seagoing steamers of a hundred feet or so in length. These killing vessels are usually known as "Whale-boats" or "Killer boats," their business being to provide the shore stations or floating factories with all the whales they can handle.

When a whale is sighted it is followed by the steamer until an opportunity for a shot is found. The harpoon is large and heavy, often weighing well over a hundred pounds and armed with four long, hinged flukes that fold to the shank while the weapon is in the gun. The head of the harpoon is fitted with an explosive bomb that is fired with a five second fuse, to give it plenty of time to enter deep into the body of the whale before the explosion takes place.

A heavy manila line, with a breaking strain of from fifteen to twenty-eight tons, is attached to the harpoon, the rope being of sufficient strength to tow the steamer after it has been made fast to the whale.

When the animal is finally killed, sometimes after a long and weary chase, the carcass is towed by the whale-boat to the shore station, or floating factory, as the case may be, where it is hauled up a slide to the cutting platform by a power windlass, and every part of the animal saved. The chief products are whalebone, oil, bone meal, flesh and fertilizer scrap. In the old, deep-sea style of whaling, the blubber-freed carcass was a total loss. Shore-whaling depends for its success on the availability of the faster-swimming baleen whales that carry much shorter "bone" and a much smaller amount of oil than do the Bowhead and Right Whale of the old-time whalers.

The Blue Whale, the Finner and the Humpback, more particularly the first two, are the species chiefly taken by the Antarctic whalers.

In 1932, A. G. Bennett, in his book, "Whaling in the Antarctic," makes the statement that 180,000 Blue, Finback and Humpback Whales were known to have been killed in the Antarctic in the 25 preceding years, which is at the rate of 7,200 a year. This would make it appear that whales were then still a long way from becoming extinct, though such extensive and continued slaughter may even now call for a modification of the statement.

The Blue Whale is the largest known form of animal life, living or extinct. Abnormally large individuals, in the Antarctic, at least, attain a length of at least 100 feet.

The Finner Whale, or Finback, reaches a length of more than seventy feet, and is more slenderly-built than the preceding species. It is probably the most abundant of the larger whales, and it is the one most frequently found washed up on the beach. It has not infrequently been found stranded at points along the North Carolina coast.

The Humpback is particularly noticeable for the abnormal length of its flippers, which measure about one third of the total length of the animal. The average length of adults of this species is about 45 feet.

The Bowhead and Right Whale usually have a maximum length of less than sixty feet, a few feet over fifty being about the maximum for the Right Whale.

Noticeable among the toothed-whale section of the whales is the fact that it contains species that have the greatest number of teeth and the smallest number of teeth of any animals of the mammalian class. At one end is the Narwhal, with only one developed tooth and at the other end the Long-beaked Dolphin that may have as many as 250 teeth.

In the case of the Narwhal the single tooth that is developed is almost invariably on the left-hand side, in the form of a long, spirally-grooved tusk, that reaches a length of seven or eight feet. Quite rarely, however, the tusk on the right side is developed equally with the other. The twist of the spiral groove is always left-handed.

Perhaps the most deadly and ferocious known mammal is the Killer Whale—often known simply as "Killer." In the vast expanses of the oceans of the world, the great Sperm Whale is the only mammal safe from the attacks of this insatiable Killer. As a whale it is not large, reaching a maximum length of about 30 feet. But it is fast, active and fearless, with a mouth full of most effective teeth, and not even the great Bowhead and Right Whales are immune from its ferocious attacks. The largest whale has no chance in a battle with two or three Killers. Aiming at the throat and lips of their victim, they tear off masses of flesh in their greed to reach the fat and juicy tongue of their victim, which seems to be their chief aim. Dolphins, porpoises and seals, even a young walrus, fall a prey to their wolfish attacks, and it has been recorded that there was once taken from the stomach of a single Killer the bodies of 13 porpoises and 14 seals. That is what I should be inclined to call a Square Meal.

A smaller, closely allied species is known as the False Killer, the food of which consists mainly of cuttlefish. This latter animal seems to possess none of the blood-thirsty characteristics of its larger relative.

The whalebone, previously mentioned as a characteristic of the Whalebone Whales, consists of a large series of horny (not bone) plates that grow downwards and outwards from the upper jaw of the animal, their inside thin edges being developed in the form of long, hair-like fibers, the whole series being enclosed by the wall-like lips of the lower jaw when the mouth is closed.

The Bowhead and Right Whales carry something like 350 to 370 of these laminae on each side of the mouth. This mass of lamina—or plates—constitutes a very perfect strainer. The whale swims slowly through the masses of small crustacea, etc. that constitute its food, lower jaw hanging low. When sufficient food for a swallow has been accumulated, the mouth is closed—the great tongue virtually filling the mouth cavity—the water gushing out between the plates of whalebone, leaving the food inside. It is then, of course, swallowed.

All the whalebone whales have comparatively small throats limited, possibly, to the passage of a fish of a few pounds weight.

The character of the food mentioned above applies more particularly to the Bowhead and Right Whales, the Finback group —which includes the Blue Whale, the Finback, the California Gray—being partial to some of the smaller fishes that travel in large schools.

The Sperm Whale seems to feed almost exclusively on cuttlefish that it finds and kills in the black depths of the various oceans. From various statements relating to this feeding habit of the Sperm Whale, it would seem that from regurgitated masses of stomach contents and from sections found adrift or ashore, this whale finds and feeds upon very much larger specimens of cuttlefish than have ever been otherwise recorded.

The Pygmy Sperm Whale—*Kogia*—is a much smaller species which, like its larger relative, has teeth only in the lower jaw.

The Beaked Whales are not far from the two foregoing species in their physical characteristics, but are smaller in size. The Bottle-nose Whales, *Hyperoodon,* are members of this group, being the only members of the group that have been hunted commercially. All the other Beaked Whales, perhaps a dozen or so species in all, are among the rarest of the whole whale family, some of them being represented as accepted records by not more than ten specimens, or less. Like the Sperm Whales, what teeth they have are confined to the lower jaw but they are few in number and some of them peculiar in either shape or placement. None has more than two pairs of teeth and some only one pair. These are much more highly developed in the male than in the female and, as the different species are largely determined by the character and placement of their teeth, the females being more difficult to place than the males.

In the case of the female specimen that was stranded on the beach below Oregon Inlet last month, no teeth showed above the gums and it was only after digging down into tissue-filled sockets at the tip of the jaws that two small teeth were finally found embedded about an inch below the surface of the gums. These were quite small, about a quarter of an inch wide, and pointed directly forward.

This specimen measured 17 feet in length, the depth of the body at its greatest circumference being about 3½ feet. Its estimated weight was about 2500 pounds. It proved to be the very rare True's Beaked Whale, of which only eight specimens have been recorded since the late Dr. F. W. True named the type specimen that was found on Bird Shoal, Beaufort Harbor, in 1912.

Our specimen contained a well-developed foetus that measured 7 feet 2 inches in length and was estimated to weigh about 175 lbs. We have this foetus preserved in fluid and a model of the parent as well as the foetus was later prepared for the N. C. State Museum from measurements, photographs and plaster casts of the head, tail and fins.

Just a few words on the Porpoises and Dolphins. And please note here that it is most unfortunate that the same name should be given to both a fish and a mammal, the name Dolphin and also the name Blackfish here relating to the mammals.*

Both the Blackfish and the Short-finned Blackfish have been taken on our coasts. Our most abundant species of this group, however, is the Common Porpoise or Bottle-nosed Dolphin. Much more rare, being more a creature of the open sea than the coastal waters, is the Common Dolphin.

We have a record of one specimen each of False Killer Whale and Harbor Porpoise. The list of species of the Whale family recorded from North Carolina waters numbers about thirteen in all. In addition, we have good evidence of the presence of the Killer Whale as sight records.

Up to half a century ago, or less, commercial whaling was

* Since vernacular or common names of animals often vary in different localities, the scientific names of whales mentioned in the present article are listed below, following the nomenclature of Anthony, *Field Book of North American Mammals* (G. P. Putnam's Sons), in order to aid the reader in looking up further information. Whalebone whales: Blue, *Sibbaldus musculus;* Bowhead, *Balaena mysticetus;* Right, *Eubalaena glacialis;* Finback, *Balænoptera physalus;* Humpback, *Megaptera nodosa;* California Gray, *Rhachianectes glaucus.* Toothed whales: Sperm, *Physeter catodom;* Narwhal, *Monodon monoceros;* Long-beaked Dolphin, *Steno rostratus;* Common Dolphin, *Delphinus delphis;* Common Porpoise, *Tursiops truncatus;* Blackfish, *Glabicephala melæna;* short-finned Blackfish, *Glabicephala brachyptera;* Harbor Porpoise, *Phocæna phocœna;* White, *Delphinapterus leucas;* Killer, *Orcinus orca;* False Killer, *Pseudorca crassidens;* True's Beaked, *Mesoplodon mirum.*—Editor

conducted locally on the North Carolina coast on a small scale for a great many years. The only species sought was the Right Whale, and the season in which the whale was pursued was in the spring, when a migration up the coast seemed to bring the animals inshore in the region of Cape Lookout and Beaufort Inlet. Perhaps half a dozen completely equipped whale-boats were kept in readiness in that region.

We have the complete equipment actually used by one of those Beaufort Harbor Whale-boats, in the Museum, one of the harpoons shown having been used in the capture of 29 whales.

I had some interesting experiences with one whale those boys had killed and which I went down to investigate; it turned out to be a Right Whale, of which the Museum already had a larger specimen. After getting back home the idea occurred to me that it might be a ripe and fruity personal gamble to have the bones of the skeleton roughed out with the idea of selling them to some museum in need of a specimen. My brother, C. S. Brimley, went in with me and together we acquired one of the most smelly collections of half-cleaned bones of a forty-four foot Right Whale of which I have direct knowledge. But when it came to shipping them to Raleigh complications developed. The railway people wanted them classified as "whalebone," a commodity then worth about $5.00 a pound and carrying a prohibitive freight rate. Following a rather long-drawn-out correspondence, I finally persuaded the railroad people to take them under the classification of "fertilizer material"—and their odor certainly indicated a very rich brand of this commodity. Storing them in Raleigh was another problem but we finally sold them to the Museum of the University of Iowa where I learned later that the mounted specimen was on display and credited to the coast of New Jersey! But as the Director of that Museum happened to be a personal friend of mine I showed him the correspondence with the University officials that related to the transfer, and the proper locality was substituted.

Up to about the time that Dr. Roy Chapman Andrews published his book, *Whale Hunting with Gun and Camera,* in 1916, whales in general had been considered animals of a slow growth, maturity only being reached after quite a long period of years. In his investigations of the whale fisheries of Japan, which began about 1910, he reached the conclusion that the great Sperm Whale reaches maturity in three or four years. Norman and Fraser, in their book, *Giant Fishes, Whales and Dolphins,* published in London in 1938, state that maturity is usually reached in the Blue Whale in two years, so it might be logical to conclude that other large whales reach maturity at a much earlier age than had formerly been supposed. This book also makes the statement that the Blue Whale reaches its full growth in 12 to 14 years.

Dr. Andrews also states in his aforementioned work on whaling that he examined the foetus of a Blue Whale that measured 25 feet in length and was estimated to weigh 8 tons. This might fill all requirements for classification as a *Bouncing Baby!*

From several specimens of Blue Whales that have been actually weighed, a hundred foot specimen would weigh about 130 tons.

No paper on whales could be considered complete without some mention of ambergris. This extremely valuable substance—10 to 15 dollars or more per ounce—is developed in the intestines of the Sperm Whale, apparently the result of a diseased condition. It is sometimes found in situ, at other times floating in the ocean or cast up on the beach. It is used as a fixative in the manufacture of perfumes. And, considering everything, it is perhaps just as well that Sperm Whale chitterlings are not highly recommended as an article of human diet!

Old-Time Whaling
in North Carolina*

Wᴴɪʟᴇ ᴡʜᴀʟɪɴɢ was never a major activity in North Carolina waters, it was, up to thirty or forty years ago, a source of a certain amount of additional income to the fishermen of the Cape Lookout region during a rather slack season in their regular occupation of fishing. But, beyond that, I have always believed that the thrills and excitement accompanying the chase and capture of these monsters of the deep had a great deal to do with the regularity with which those hardy coastdwellers made ready for the chase year after year as the days of early spring rolled around.

It has been my good fortune to have been more or less closely associated with six individual whales, five of them either killed or stranded in the general vicinity of Cape Lookout. Four of these were Right Whales and one a Finback, the sixth being the big bull Sperm Whale that stranded on Wrightsville Beach in

* A revision of a paper published in *The American Angler*, XXV, No. 3 (March, 1895), 67-75. The drawings by Frank Greene in this and the preceding article appeared in the original publication.

the spring of 1928. The skeletons of three of these—a Right, a Finback and a Sperm—are now on exhibition in the State Museum.

The first recognition of whales as a valuable product of the coastal waters of North Carolina of which I have knowledge is contained in a lease made between the Lords Proprietors and Mr. Burrington *et al.*, dated May 29, 1723, the original lease being in the State Hall of History. This lease provides for (the following being a quotation from the lease): "fishing, and taking of all sorts of Whales, Sturgeons and other Royall fish whatsoever upon the northern part of the province of Carolina aforesaid (that is to say) between the river Cape Fare and Curratuck Inlett ... from the Feast Day of the Blessed Virgin Mary next coming." (End of quotation).

It would be interesting to know how many whales were taken by Mr. Burrington *et al.* under this lease!

On August 3, 1926, I had a most enjoyable visit from my old friend, Captain John E. Lewis, of Morehead City. We talked mainly about the old-time whaling in the region of Cape Lookout, and I asked a great many questions on the subject, as I have for many years wanted to write up something of permanent value on the history of the whaling industry in North Carolina. But it seems very difficult to secure any reliable data regarding its origin, and its history for the first century or so of its existence.

It was a habit of our whaling crews to give names to a good many of the whales caught, particularly the larger ones. One was named "The Little Children," for the reason that the boats taking it were manned mainly by boys, the older members of the families not being available at the time. The Right Whale whose skeleton hangs in the Museum was called the "Mayflower," for reasons given me by Captain Lewis.

You must understand that virtually all of the whales killed on our coast were Right Whales, the only other species at all common being the Finback, a species of little or no commercial value, this whale often exceeding the former species in length, though not in bulk.

Soon after his return home, Captain Lewis collected such facts beyond his own knowledge that he could dig up and embodied them in a letter to me under date of September 18, 1926. I am quoting his letter in full, as it carries the proper salty flavor in addition to the facts presented. Here it is:

"My dear Mr. Brimley: In complying with your request I have collected the following facts about the killing of the whale Mayflower, which occurred about 1874.

"He was named 'Mayflower' by the men who killed him because he was killed the fourth of May. He was one of the biggest ever killed in these parts, and perhaps the most vicious, since it took fully half a day to kill him.

"There were six boats in action, containing six men each; four men rowing, with the captain in the head, directing, and the steersman in the stern taking orders and steering the boat. The captain, in the head, always shot the guns and threw the harpoons. The following are the names of the captains of the boats who helped kill this particular whale: Elsie Guthrie, W. C. Guthrie, James Lewis, Samuel Windsor, Josephus Willis, Reuben Willis.

"None of the captains are living. Out of the crews there are but three living, and they are Sam Lewis, Bill Guthrie and Billy Willis.

"The whale came in the hook (this means the hook or Bight of Cape Lookout) that morning, soon, and all six boats headed for him. Captain Reuben Willis was the first to strike him with the shackle (this means the type of harpoon usually called a 'toggle-iron') and then the big fight began.

"All the guns were shot and he had to be finally killed with the irons and harpoons.

"He fought and slashed about at the six boats for hours, they laying off to one side, and whenever a captain in either boat could pick a chance when his tail was not slashing in his direction, he would rush in and harpoon him.

"One of the crew, Absalom Guthrie, kept an account of the number of whales that he and Mr. James Lewis helped kill, and it was fifty-two. This number, of course, was of those killed during his generation.

"The writer has since that time, during his generation, helped kill ten.

"There were two generations before Absalom's time, and we don't know how many were killed then.

"During this third generation, all the whalemen, along towards the last few years of their activities, amalgamated, forming one big fighting unit, which tended more towards efficiency and returned them more money per capita.

"These six crews were all the whalemen in eastern North Carolina.

"It was a hard and dangerous life, but was so thrilling and fascinating that it seemed to grip and hold the men, so that once a whaleman, always a whaleman.

"Whales still come here almost like they used to, but they are no longer hunted as of old. Other things have crowded in which are more remunerative, and the industry declined about twenty-five years ago.

"I take great pleasure in presenting these facts for your consideration, and remain, Yours very truly, Captain John E. Lewis." (End of Captain Lewis' letter).

"Once a whaleman, always a whaleman," reflects the attitude of those men. I have talked with a number of them in years gone by and, believe me, they always proved a fine bunch of fellows. Meeting up with Redheaded Joe Lewis on Shackleford's Banks that time I was dickering for the skeleton of the Mullet Pond whale, I found Joe with a slab of skin missing from his nose. No, Joe hadn't been in a fight, the recoil of one of those heavy whale guns being responsible for the missing skin. He had merely been assisting in the killing of a whale!

On March 20, 1894, these whalers killed a big cow whale off Wade Shore, a small settlement on Shackleford's Banks about four miles east of Beaufort Inlet, finishing the job about ten miles out to sea. You can imagine what a back-breaking job the oarsmen of these five boats had in towing the enormous carcass to the beach. There were no helpful gas engines in those days, sails or oars doing all the local transportation work on the water, at least where steam tugs were not handy.

I took measurements of this whale on the spot. It was fifty-three feet long, its lower jawbones each measured fourteen feet around

bove, A great Sperm Whale washed up on a North Carolina beach. As with most whales *he* mouth is relatively small, and these giants of nature feed on small forms of ocean life. *elow,* Mr. Brimley working on a model of True's Beaked Whale, a small but very rare *hale. (Both, N. C. State Museum)*

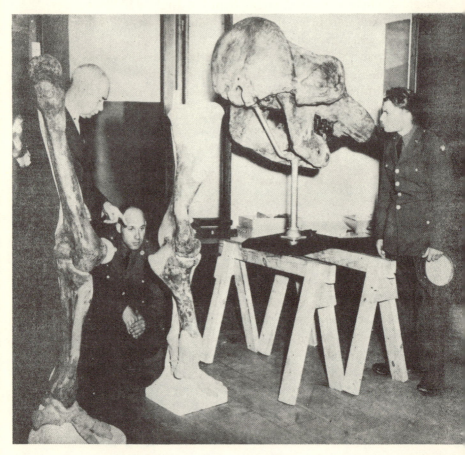

Mr. Brimley showing servicemen the remains of great mammoths which once roamed North Carolina. These remains are now in the State Museum, Raleigh, North Carolina. (*N. C. State Museum*)

the curve; from eye to tip of upper jaw, twelve feet, and the flukes of the tail were seventeen feet across. These measurements indicate a whale somewhat larger than the Right whale we have in the Museum and bring it close to being the largest whale of this species ever taken on our coast.

The oil from this specimen amounted to about 39 barrels, and the whalebone to 864 pounds, the latter selling for $1.65 a pound. The oil sold for twenty-five cents a gallon, the total value of the products amounting to slightly over $1,900, which was quite a sizable bunch of money in those days.

The whale "fishery" on our coast was always cooperative, as it was in the old deep-sea whale fisheries operating from New Bedford and Nantucket, i.e. every man engaged in any particular chase sharing equally in the proceeds after certain fixed charges had been paid. The data relating to the shares, or "lays," as they were sometimes called, given me at the killing of this last-mentioned whale, were as follows: each gun drew two shares, one share went to the owner of each boat; each full set of tackle —harpoons, lances, warps, drags, boat-spades, etc.—drew two-thirds of a share, while the harpooner and steersman of each boat drew the other third of the tackle share.

The men actually in the boats participating in the chase, whether regular members of the crew, or not, each drew one share. Besides the above distribution of the proceeds of the catch, there was a charge of five gallons of oil to the owner of each kettle used in trying out the oil.

The taking of this big whale showed a total of 44 shares, so, each man participating received slightly over $43. To say nothing of the fun involved!

A smaller whale had been killed off Cape Lookout a day or two before this big fellow came to hand, and several others had been unsuccessfully chased within the previous month or so. Yes, they used to kill whales around Cape Lookout!

Trying out the oil from the blubber is real work and is not highly recommended as an indoor recreation on a rainy day. The blubber, a delicate salmon-pink in color, is stripped off the carcass in blocks about as large as two men can carry handily. A hole is cut through the block near one end, a pole is stuck through the hole, the pole is shouldered by a couple of men, who carry it to the mincing trough. Here, a mincing knife—which may be made from an old scythe blade—is used in cutting it up in thin strips, which are fed to the try-pots.

Cutting Blubber.

The try-pots are iron kettles of about fifty gallons capacity, temporarily set up in brick-work, and the fires are fed mainly with the cracklings, these consisting of the crisp, oily residue of the blubber after the oil has been extracted.

Trying Out Oil.

The combination of odors from a smelly whale carcass on the beach with the sickening effluvia of boiling oil, together with the aroma of burning grease from the fires, is hard to beat from an olfactory standpoint. Those working in it didn't seem to mind it at all, perhaps for the reason that "familiarity breeds contempt," but, so far as I was concerned, I distinctly remember that I did not have much appetite for supper that night!

Sharks I Have Known—And Others*

The shark is not often the subject
   Of poetry—real or near
It seems to me time that his shark-ship
   In one rhyme at least should appear;
So here is my humble endeavor
   To give him his dues and be fair
To all his good points—if he has them—
   Including his fishy-eyed stare.

He is not the insatiable eater
   Of man, that they'd have you believe:
His records are scanty—or absent—
   Of causing the widow to grieve
The loss of her dear late lamented;
   In fact, he would rather eat fish
Than menfolk or women or children—
   And mostly he follows his wish.

* Unpublished manuscript written about 1935, except for the poem which was originally printed in the *Charlotte Observer*.

I will not deny that he is wolfish
  And often kills more than he needs;
But then again, this is done often
  By men of all nations and creeds.
He is careful to fill up his stomach
  When tasty food crosses his path,
For the next meal is always uncertain
  And he don't care to look like a lath

Of course you have heard of the monster
  Cut open upon the ship's deck,
Wherein the crew found several seamen
  Pulled down from a water-logged wreck,
All seated and playing at setback
  For gold coins they'd found there inside—
But I think that the man who first told this
  Most ably and thoroughly lied.

He's gentle, when one gets to know him—
  Though safer to handle with care;
His teeth are as sharp as your razor
  When whetted to split a fine hair:
You'd better not be too familiar,
  Or scratch him too much on the head
And, perhaps, when it comes to a showdown
  He is safer—and better—when dead.

The idea of a shark in the water usually inspires about as much repugnance to the average person as does that of a snake on land. But when one considers the fact that perhaps ninety-nine and nine-tenths per cent of those seen, or caught in our waters on hook and line, are as harmless as a salt herring, the word "shark" should lose at least a part of its terror. There are more than sixty known species—of all degrees of size, disposition and pulchritude —found in American waters, of which perhaps twenty species occur on the North Carolina coast.

None of those recorded from our waters is considered in any

way dangerous to bathers, with possibly one exception, the so-called "Man-eater" or Great White Shark (*Carcharodon carcharias*), which is not common on the North Carolina coast. Of course, it is not well to stick a finger or a hand in the mouth of any kind of freshly caught shark just to see if it will bite, as most species are equipped with five or six rows of very sharp teeth with serrated cutting edges quite capable of shearing off the offending finger or hand, as the case might be. Besides this, a large specimen might easily slap a person over by a sweep of its powerful tail, though this would be a very humiliating method of being injured by a shark.

Sharks range in size from the little Cat Shark (*Catulus retifer*), that is only about a foot long at maturity, to the great Whale Shark (*Rhineodon typus*) which seems to reach a size approaching that of the larger whales. Both the Whale Shark and the Basking Shark (*Cetorhinus maximus*)—the latter reaching a length of about forty feet—are great, harmless, sluggish creatures, the teeth being both very small and very numerous and in no way suited for inflicting dangerous wounds.

Dr. Russell J. Coles, of Danville, Virginia, who, during the first fifteen years of the present century, did more than all other observers combined to increase our knowledge of the various species of sharks and rays frequenting the region of Cape Lookout, tells of some interesting and thrilling experiences, a number of which at times bordered on tragedy.

The boats he used in his shark investigations were always equipped with various types of harpoons, lances, and powerful rifles, which weapons he often found necessary in the pursuit of his vocation.

Doctor Coles spent long summers at Cape Lookout during the period in question. Fearless himself, he had equally fearless assistants, and the way in which he sought and tackled the great—and often little-known—fish he caught and killed—some of them potentially dangerous—is the basis of thrilling stories. I am quoting the following incident from his published writings, which describes an adventure with a species of the possibly dangerous "Man-eater" shark previously referred to:

"In 1905, while out in a small skiff harpooning turtles, a huge shark of more than twenty feet in length appeared alongside, within reach of my hand. It apparently had no fear of us as it struck the side of the skiff with some force. It then swam away for a distance of several hundred yards, then turned and swam rapidly towards us. I was about to fire into it when a large Loggerhead Turtle arose to the surface and was attacked by the shark. The shark seized the turtle in its jaws and both disappeared beneath the surface. The next day I harpooned this turtle and found the upper shell for a width of nearly thirty inches showing the marks of the shark's teeth. The edge of the shell and the right hind flipper had been torn away. In 1913, I observed three of these sharks and succeeded in harpooning them, but my tackle was too light to hold them. While I was unable to positively identify these sharks, I believe they were Man-eaters."

On another occasion—I am quoting this incident from memory —Doctor Coles was out in water between breast and waist deep, armed with a favorite harpoon, the line attached to the harpoon running to his boat that was lying off a short distance away. He also had with him a bag of "chum," consisting of ground-up fish. This, when fed slowly down the tide, seems to carry the news of food near-by to any predacious species of fish that may run into the stream of choice morsels.

A large shark, that he presumed to be a Man-eater, got the news, following up the line of chum towards its source and increasing its speed of approach as the lure became stronger. The shark finally saw the man and came on like a speedboat. At just the right time, Coles hurled the harpoon, the weapon sinking deep in the shark's body just back of its head. As the harpoon found its mark, Coles swayed on one side to avoid the direct rush of the infuriated fish, throwing up his nearest arm as a shield. The shark rushed by, catching Coles between its body and the shaft of the harpoon, breaking the latter off short and scraping the face of the harpooner with the rough, sand-paper-like skin of the fish as it passed. Coles' only criticism was that the iron should have stood the shock without breaking— and that he would have to change his harpoon maker!

The State Museum has, during the past few years, secured specimens of two species of shark very rare on our coast. The first of these was a sixteen-foot Thresher Shark (*Alopias vulpes*), taken in a net about a mile offshore from Shell Island, not far from Wrightsville Beach, and donated to the Museum by Mr. J. B. Fales, of Wilmington, whose boats secured the specimen.

The peculiar characteristic of this fish, from which it takes its name, is its enormously long tail. Our specimen, sixteen feet in length, has seven and a half feet devoted to head and body and eight and a half feet to its tail. The tail is used for stunning or killing the fish on which it feeds, and the three specimens recorded as having been caught by anglers in the Catalina region of the California coast were all hooked in the tail! Romer Gray caught a specimen—hooked in the mouth, this time—about fifteen feet in length while fishing for swordfish in Australian waters a few years ago. This species does not seem to be common anywhere.

The tails of all sharks are heterocercal, that is, the caudal vertebrae are continued in an upward direction from the point at which they normally end, this producing an elongation of the upper lobe of the tail fin. This elongation is carried out to an extreme degree in the Thresher Shark, as indicated in the comparative length of tail compared with that of the head and body, as noted above.

Dr. Coles records a specimen seen near Cape Lookout in 1913, and another in 1914. But the Museum Thresher Shark seems to be the only specimen recorded as actually captured in North Carolina waters.

Two or three years ago, Mr. and Mrs. Frank Bennett, of Durham, N. C., were fishing for Sea Trout (Weakfish) in Bogue Sound, just west of the causeway, using the regulation light tackle prescribed for this class of fishing, with a number two hook on the line. Mrs. Bennett hooked a fish and started pulling it in when, suddenly, the line stopped as if caught in some obstruction—and then started running out. Mrs. Bennett, realizing that something heavier than she cared to handle was on her line, called on her husband—an experienced fisherman—for assistance. Mr. Bennett took the line and, by careful manipulation, he finally brought the fish to the surface. When it appeared, it proved to be something unknown to the boatman, so every care was taken not to lose it. There was no gaff in the boat, and no firearm of any kind with which to kill it, but a hammer was found and the fish was whaled over the head the next time it was brought sufficiently near the boat. The first blow, however, while somewhat quieting the fish's energies, had been too far forward and Mr. Bennett had to give the line and play his quarry further before again bringing it alongside.

The second lick with the hammer—directly on the base of the skull—did the trick, and the fish was hauled into the boat, but it had to be taken to the Marine Biological Laboratory at Beaufort for identification. It proved to be a Nurse Shark (*Ginglymostoma cirratum*), measuring 5½ feet in length and weighing 55 pounds.

A small fish had evidently taken the hook first, and the shark took the first fish while it was on its way to the boat.

The Nurse Shark is common in tropical waters, but very rare on our coast. Doctor Coles records seeing a school of these sharks on Lookout shoals in the summer of 1913. He hooked a ninefooter and brought it alongside his boat; but, in attempting to kill it, his lance rebounded from the thick, tough, pebbly hide, and he had to file his lance-blade to a very sharp point before he succeeded in killing his specimen, of which only the head was preserved. This was the first record of this species in our waters, and our Museum specimen seems to be the second.

Mr. Wendell Endicott, in his book, *Adventures with Rod and Harpoon Along the Florida Keys,* mentions the difficulty in making even the sharpest of harpoons penetrate the skin of this species. The skin, on the back, particularly, is thick, tough, and has the appearance of being inlaid with small, round pebbles. It is awfully hard on the knives used in skinning a specimen.

The Nurse Shark is not a dangerous species, the teeth being very small for the size of the fish.

There are two sharks occurring more or less commonly on our coast that are remarkable for the peculiar shape of their heads, these being the Bonnet-headed Shark (*Sphyrna tiburo*), and the Hammerhead (*Sphyrna zygaena*).

The Bonnet-head is a comparatively small species, not usually exceeding five feet in length. The head is broad and rounded in front and very much flattened and extended at the sides, its shape when viewed from above being very similar to that of a shovel blade with a rounded edge.

The Hammerhead reaches a length of fifteen feet, or more, and its head is one of the most peculiar among fishes. The head is widely extended at the sides beyond the line of the neck, the general appearance as seen from above being that of the head of a sledge hammer, the neck of the fish representing the handle. A specimen eleven feet long had a head thirty inches wide, with a neck of about eight inches in width. And, to add to the odd appearance of the creature, the eyes are set in the ends of the extended parts of the head. In fact, one measures from eye to eye in ascertaining the widest part of the head. A big Hammerhead is a bad boy to tackle on a line!

Just a few more words about the Whale Shark. Several specimens of this very rare and enormous creature—which is the largest of all fishes—have been taken in Florida waters. At least one of these—possibly, two—was embalmed or otherwise preserved, mounted on a flat car, and taken around the country for exhibit purposes.

Mack Sennett, while fishing from his yacht off the southern point of California, a few years ago, was in contact with a specimen that he estimated to measure sixty feet in length. He secured pictures of the animal, but from his account of the incident the fish did not register either alarm or undue excitement when attacked with harpoons and other lethal weapons.

In North Carolina waters our commonest species of shark are, possibly, the Sand Shark (*Carcharias littoralis*) and the Sharp-nosed Shark (*Scoliodon terrae-novae*), particularly the former. This species is comparatively easy to identify by the very long, narrow teeth, most of the teeth being equipped with cusps at their base. But the identification of sharks by their teeth alone, I have found a difficult proposition, as the diagnostic characters of this group of fishes are based largely on the position, shape and comparative size of the fins. The comparative size, number and position of the gill openings are also used as identification marks.

The skeletons of all sharks are cartilaginous, and this is the reason that fossil remains of members of this group are mainly confined to their teeth.

A good many years ago, a specialized variety of leather was made from shark-skin that was known as Shagreen. This leather had a pebbly surface that was secured by drying it with a quantity of small, hard, round seeds that had been embedded on the reverse side while it was moist. It was dyed green, a mottled effect being secured by the impression of the seeds locally altering the density of the fibers in a way that caused it to absorb the dye in varying degrees of strength.

During the war (1919), methods of preparing shark leather suitable for shoes were developed, the organized taking of sharks being established at various places along our coasts, one of which operated on the beach near Beaufort, N. C.*

Two methods of reproduction are found among sharks, some species laying eggs and others bringing forth their young alive.

Here are a few more or less intimate associations with sharks that may pave the way to a better understanding of these interesting creatures:

Some friends of mine were fishing for Red Drum in the surf near Topsail Inlet, in Pender County. The drum were plentiful, cutting at a school of mullets, and some sharks had rallied around to feed on the drum. Directly in front of one of the men a breaking wave brought a thirty-pound drum up the beach with a good sized shark in close pursuit. As the wave washed the two fish up the slope of sand, the shark caught the drum and swallowed it as he came, but was left stranded close to the fisherman's feet as the wave receded. Having no weapon at hand, he

---

*In the Second World War sharks were again exploited because the liver oils of some species have a high Vitamin A content.—Editor

poked the shark in the slats with the butt-end of his fishing rod —when another wave broke, rolled up the beach and took the shark with it back to the sea. That particular shark was evidently an efficiency expert.

I got rather a calling down one day on this shark question. My wife and I were surf-fishing. She had waded out and made a cast seaward, and was standing in the water, with her back to the shore, perhaps sixty or seventy-five yards from the line of beach. As soon as I had rigged up my tackle, I waded out in the general line she had taken when, suddenly, a fair-sized shark appeared between us, crossing her line of travel. I stopped and made a quick cast in front of the swimming fish in the hope that he would see the bait and take hold, but the act failed to register. My calling down was based on the stated belief that I had stopped to try to hook and have some sport with a ferocious man-eating creature that might have eaten up my lady friend while I was simply fishing for fun. I found it difficult to get my scientific explanations received in the right spirit.

Exactly what sense organ or organs it is in fish that corresponds to nasal membranes in air-breathing animals is not clear, but I *do* know that sharks have a "keen sense of smell." One day, at the Topsail Inlet fishing camp, I picked up a gray sea-trout that had been overlooked by the cook and become rather smelly and pitched it into the water of the sound. My throw was rather short and the fish lay partly in the water and partly out. A little later I went down to the edge of the water for something and noticed the fish lying there. I was about to kick it out into the tideway when I accidentally happened to see the dorsal fin of a shark about 150 yards down the run of the tide from where I was standing, the fin quartering back and forth across the current but generally heading towards me. It suddenly dawned on me that this shark boy was after the spoiled trout, so I watched the fin with renewed interest.

As it came nearer, the zigzagging toned down to a straight course and the speed of the fin increased. Up the tide the shark came, turned in sharp when opposite the dead fish, grabbed it—

though he had to stick his head out of the water to do it—and another shark had earned his supper by hunting for it.

Almost immediately after this interesting experience, another shark fin was seen just about where the first one had originally come into view, and this one followed the line of scent almost exactly as the first had done. You ought to have seen the disgusted "expression" on the face of shark number two when he found nothing to eat at the end of his quest!

One morning down at the Onslow Club, a couple of fishermen had brought in a nice string of fish, among them being a large black bass and a rather fine example of striped bass, the latter being an unusual take in those waters.

These two had been left on a stringer hanging overboard from the canoe from which they had been caught—the canoe swinging off from the dock in front of the house—so as to keep them alive to show to other fishermen as they came in.

While sitting on the front porch of the clubhouse overlooking the broad expanse of water directly in front, I happened to remark that I did not remember having seen a shark around there for several years. Within five minutes after making that statement, the unmistakable triangular dorsal fin of one appeared some sixty or seventy yards beyond the dock from which the canoe was swinging.

I jumped for my rifle, which was just inside the house, picked up three or four cartridges and ran down the steps and along the dock, loading the magazine of the rifle as I ran. When I had reached a point on the dock just beyond where the canoe lay, the fin of the shark was much closer in, still quartering backwards and forwards across the end of the dock, when it suddenly came to me that he was following up the light "scent" of the two fish on the string.

A cabin gas boat was tied up on the right-hand side of the dock near its farther end and when the shark's fin went out of view behind it, now pretty close in, I got ready to shoot as soon as it appeared again from behind the gas boat. But it didn't appear where and when and how I expected.

Just after the fin went out of my line of vision, the shark evidently caught the direct line of scent in sufficient strength to indicate the nearness of its prospective meal and its definite position, and he came into full view from beneath the gas boat and almost under my feet, coming like a torpedo. I don't know now whether I had time to get the gun to my shoulder or whether I just pointed it at him as I pulled the trigger, but I loosed two high-powered bullets just as fast as I could crook my trigger finger twice, the rifle being of the automatic type.

With a water shield approximately a foot thick between me and the shark's body, I failed to score a hit—but I saved the fish on the stringer, while the shark departed for parts unknown.

The water in which this incident happened was almost devoid of current, and yet the scent of those two fish tied to the canoe had been disseminated over such a wide area that it finally reached the olfactory organs of that particular shark nearly a hundred yards away.

Mammoths and Mastodons in North Carolina*

From the depths of the peat of the swamp fed creek,
  Where the great dredge eats its way,
There were brought some bones of the Mammoth vast
  To the light of a modern day.

From the place where the huge beast found his rest,
  In the days when the world was young,
Ere the First Man's track in the mud was made,
  Or his spear to the winds was flung:

When the hairy brute, of a strength untold,
  Roamed alone through the swamps and reeds;
Razed the cane-breaks dense, tramped the gall bush down,
  In the place where the bear now feeds.

* Unpublished manuscript written about 1929, except for the poem which is reprinted from *North Carolina Poems*, edited by E. C. Brooks, published by North Carolina Education, Raleigh, N. C., 1912.

When his long trunk rose in the quivering air,
　　And his tusks 'neath the moon gleamed white,
And his trumpet call through the woodlands rang
　　In the hush of the cool swamp night.

And an answering call to his war cry bold
　　Through the isles of the wood rang shrill—
'Twas the battle cry of the Mastodon,
　　From the place where he drank his fill.

Fierce rivals, these, for the Woodland's Rule—
　　And they fought ere the night was done:
And a deep, dark pool in the cypress swamp
　　Made a grave for the vanquished one.

Like great freight trains, on a down-hill grade,
　　With the weights piled ton on ton,
Came the Mammoth vast, in his charging rush—
　　Came the mighty Mastodon.

And they met with a crash that the swamp-lands shook—
　　And the wood-folk cowered in awe;
They met like ships in a head-on clash
　　In their fight 'neath the Woodland Law.

And the trees went down in the conflict fierce,
　　And the ground was plowed and raw;
For they fought a fight where to lose meant death—
　　And the thick reeds gave like straw.

Then the wound-forced screams of the huge mad beasts
　　Through the swamp mists rose and fell,
With their notes of rage and their notes of fear
　　Like the screams of the fiends in Hell.

And their tusks gored deep and their wounds gaped wide,
　　And the spouting blood ran free,
Till their strength was gone, and their lives ebbed fast
　　As they still fought, knee to knee

Above, Ocean Sunfish, *Mola mola,* caught at Swansboro, May, 1926. This is the specimen from which the model in the State Museum was made. *Below,* putting the finishing touches on the model. (*Both, N. C. State Museum*)

One of the largest Black Marlins taken on the Carolina coast. Weight, 593 pounds
(*N. C. State Museum*)

Model of the Nurse Shark as now exhibited in the State Museum.
(*N. C. State Museum*)

Head of the Basking Shark. (*N. C. State Museum*)

Till the vanquished died—and the victor too—
And their forms in the pool sank deep,
To be peat-wrapped there—till the great dredge brought
Their remains from their last long sleep.

In approaching the subject of the occurrence of the mammoth and the mastodon in North Carolina, it is necessary first to discuss the relationship of these animals to modern forms of life, and also to present some facts relating to their general characteristics and to their former distribution over the various countries of the earth.

Our knowledge of the occurrence of these great beasts of the past in North Carolina is very definite, though somewhat fragmentary since fossil records are rarely complete. Both the mammoths and the mastodons—there being a number of species of each—belong to the order Ungulata, hoofed animals; sub-order Proboscidea,* animals with a trunk. In fact, the present-day elephants and the mammoths are so closely related as to be included in the same genus—*Elephas*.

The scientific name of the sub-order is based on the presence of a proboscis, or trunk. And it is well to consider this point, that no human mind could ever have imagined such an unusual and so highly-specialized a nose as is the elephant's trunk. Think of this point for a moment. Suppose that a number of other representative groups of mammals were known to you—giraffes, field mice, whales, rabbits, cows, hound dogs, bats, hippopotami, kangaroos, etc. Consider the nasal development of any of these, and then try to reason from your own knowledge that there might be some related species with a nose so developed that it could perform the following functions: Draw water from a pool at the owner's feet with the head seven or eight feet above the ground; fill itself with water and then discharge its contents into the underlying mouth—its only method of drinking; pick up a tiny object off the ground, or tear down a medium-sized tree; knock out an enemy with a single blow; give the whole of the

* More recent classifications give the Proboscidea the rank of a full order, separate from the true hoofed mammals (cattle, deer, etc.).—Editor

owner's body either a dust- or shower-bath; gather food for its owner, the only means by which he can be fed; catch the scent of an enemy from air layers close to the ground, or twelve feet above the ground level. It is utterly beyond any power of human imagination to picture such a nose—without actual knowledge thereof.

The only feeding done by an elephant without the aid of the trunk is during the nursing period, the baby elephants taking their nourishment directly through the lips, with the little trunk curled up out of the way.

Now for some relationships: The mastodons are probably of a more remote type than the mammoths. One of the earliest known forms of large elephant was the Dinotherium, with molar teeth very similar to those of the mastodons, and with two tusks in the lower jaw. This pair of tusks pointed downward, almost at right angles to the line of the jaw. The earlier investigators of the lower jaws of this animal—the only part at that time known —classified them as belonging to some marine monster, there being no associated bones available by which the true relationship could be determined. The original stock from which the Proboscidea have been presumedly derived is represented by Moeritherium, a small animal with small tusks and numerous teeth supposed to have lived in the Eocene.

Coming to the mastodons proper, we find the tusks of the upper jaw well developed, and much on a par with those of the elephants of the present day. In some species, a pair of smaller tusks is carried in the lower, but never at the expense of the upper-jaw tusks. It may be noted here that the normal upper-jaw tusks of the members of the elephant group are modifications of two of the incisor teeth, and not of the canine teeth, as one might expect them to be.

The elephants in general have only one or two functional molar or jaw teeth on each side of each jaw. But the character of the molar teeth in the mastodons and the mammoths is very different. The molars of all the mastodons have cross ridges and depressions like miniature mountain ranges and valleys, on the grinding surface, while the faces of the corresponding teeth of the mammoths—and of the modern elephants—are flat, with the cross ridges of the enamel only slightly raised above the general level of the face.

Many people have the idea that the mammoth was so named on account of its great size. Almost the reverse is the case, however. In 1696, a Russian named Ludloff was told by some of the Siberian natives of a great animal whose bones were often found in the earth. As these bones were never found above ground, the natives naturally concluded that they belonged to some creature that spent its life underground, a sort of gigantic mole. In fact, for this reason they gave the animal the Tartar name Mamantu, which means earth-dweller. Coming from the Tartar language through German and then French, we get the modernized form, mammoth.

Both the mammoths and the mastodons were great hairy brutes, more imposing in appearance than the comparatively naked-skinned elephants we are accustomed to see at the circus, though a very erroneous opinion is generally held as to their size. Most of the mastodons and many of the mammoths did not average as large as a fully adult African elephant of the present day. Let that sink in! The maximum known height of an old bull African elephant is about 11½ feet at the shoulder, while many—perhaps most—of the mastodons will miss that height by a foot and a half or two feet. So far as I have been able to determine, the specimen of which we have a number of bones in the Museum measured between eight and a half and nine feet at the shoulder. The mastodons were more stockily built than the modern elephants, and it may be that our Museum specimen weighed three and a half or four tons when alive. No pet to have around the house, perhaps, and quite large enough for ordinary purposes, one might well believe.

But, some of the American mammoths, particularly the Imperial Mammoth—*Elephas imperator*—of the southern and southwestern States, were as much superior in size to the adult African elephant as that animal is to the common, or garden variety of, mastodon. With a maximum shoulder height (so far as our present knowledge goes) of thirteen—or even fourteen—feet, and with tusks in proportion, an animal of truly enormous size is indicated.

When scientific knowledge was less widely diffused than it is now, and when the science of paleontology was more or less in its infancy, the bones of these extinct elephants were regarded as belonging to giants, pagan heroes or Christian saints. One giant in particular, Teutobochus, King of the Cimbri, a bright boy of only nineteen feet in height, was suggested as the original owner of one lot of such bones. Teuto would have been bad medicine to meet on a dark night near a graveyard! Another young gentleman of Scottish descent, who went by the name of Little John, was given credit as the original owner of some of these bones, but Little John was comparatively small, only fourteen feet in his stocking feet.

An interesting point concerning the tusks of extinct elephants is that for many years a large trade in "fossil ivory" has been carried on in Siberia. This trade seems to date back to about the tenth century, and the supply seems to be by no means exhausted. Alaska and China have also contributed prehistoric ivory, it being in the main, if not entirely, made up of mammoth tusks. The delta of the Lena River is, perhaps, near the center of the territory producing this commodity. In fact, the statement has been made that many of the islands of the Lena delta are composed mainly of sand, ice, and mammoth bones.

We are so accustomed to regard the elephants as inhabitants of tropical countries that it comes almost as a shock to learn that the mammoths seemed to have reached their greatest abundance near the borders of the Arctic Ocean, in Siberia. Or, it may have been in that part of Europe now covered by the North Sea before England became an island, as great numbers of mammoth teeth have been dredged from these waters by the local fishermen. But, wherever it was, the mammoths were generously equipped for a life amidst the snow and ice of the high latitudes. While the present-day elephants are almost hairless, the mammoths were clothed in a dense covering of hair. There was a thick coat of close under-fur, or wool, with a more sparsely growing covering of longer and coarser hair that acted as a thatch in shedding the rain and snow and keeping the warmth-retaining under-fur dry. Some of the fur of mammoths that has been measured ran from a foot to a foot and a half in length, and one can image from that what sort of a fur coat could be made from mammoth hide, particularly when one considers that a very shaggy coon-skin coat carries fur that averages less than two inches in length.

An explanation of how we know anything about the body-covering of an animal that has been extinct for many thousands of years would seem to be in order.

At least four "cold-storage" mammoths have been found at different times in Siberia, not less than two of which were intact when discovered. The first of these came to light in 1799, and the skeleton of this specimen was secured by the St. Petersburg —now Leningrad—Museum. From these fresh (?) specimens we know not only the texture and length of the body-covering, but also the color of the animal when alive, which was a reddish brown.

One of the most thrilling of these discoveries of cold-storage mammoths was made in 1846 by a young Russian engineer named Benkendorf. This young chap was doing survey work in the region of the Lena and Indigirka Rivers. With a small steamer that he used in his work he was heading up the Indigirka River to meet a party of natives who were to assist him. The weather was particularly warm for a Siberian summer, heavy rains had been falling and the river was in high flood and full of tree-trunks, masses of peat and other drift. This made navigation uncertain and dangerous, but the party finally landed safely at a point where the flood waters were cutting a new channel in the river, the stream being about two miles wide at the place.

The natives he expected to meet had not arrived, so the engineer's party went into camp to await their arrival. While at work on the bank, one of Benkendorf's helpers suddenly called his attention to something in the water. The engineer turned just in time to see an enormous black head, with waving trunk and long white tusks as it sank beneath the rushing flood. After a short interval the head appeared again, rising and falling and swaying with the current, as if alive.

Benkendorf at once recognized the animal as a mammoth and, knowing that the ground in that region was permanently frozen a few feet below the surface, he realized that the flood waters had loosened and thawed the soil in which the animal's body had been frozen for untold centuries, but that the hind feet of the creature were still bound in their icy prison, temporarily anchoring the body of the great beast against the pull of the current.

Knowing that this temporary anchorage was likely to give way at any time, he had his men fasten chains and ropes to the carcass and stake them down on shore. Soon after, the native tribesmen arrived on their ponies, and the whole force of men and horses was put to work and the mammoth finally dragged out of the water.

They cut off the tusks, which were eight feet in length, and then Benkendorf had the stomach removed for an examination of its contents. Preservation was so perfect that he easily identified the most recently taken of the animal's food, which consisted of young shoots of fir and pine, together with young fir cones.

Benkendorf did not notice that the flood-water was still cutting away the bank while he was carrying on his investigations, but his work was suddenly interrupted by a cry from some of his men and a loud splash, and he turned just in time to see a large section of the bank cave in and five of his men and the body of the mammoth disappear in the swirling current. The men were rescued but the body of the mammoth was not seen again. The black color of the head was due to its hairy covering being saturated and matted with pitch, evidently accumulated while the animal was browsing among the resinous branches of pine and fir trees.

This animal had probably bogged down and frozen solid as he stood, but the date of his demise can only be guessed at. There were no birth and death registrations in his day!

More recently, another of these "cold-storage" mammoths, discovered in 1900, had met death so suddenly that when found its mouth contained food that it had been in the act of taking when it went over the precipice, or into the ice crevasse, that was presumably the cause of the animal's death, as it was found imbedded in the ice at the foot of a perpendicular river bank. The natives who found this specimen sold their rights in it to a Koblynsk Cossack officer named Javlovski. But Javlovski was taken ill before he could properly protect his purchase so it was a year later before the Russian governmental party of zoologists sent out to secure the specimen reached the place. The wild animals had devoured all of the best of the flesh and much of the skin had been torn to pieces. But they—the zoologists—secured the most perfect skeleton of a mammoth so far known. They also took out with them some large pieces of skin, bundles of wool and hair, specimens of blood and flesh, the eyes and the tail, and twenty-seven pounds of food from the stomach. One piece of the skin weighed 470 pounds, and several hundred pounds of flesh were secured. This was a rather small specimen, though no measurements are given.

As previously stated, it seems probable that the region from which the mammoth herds subsequently almost populated the earth was in northern Siberia or western Europe. Assuming the former to be more probable, they spread west and south virtually to the borders of the Atlantic and Indian Oceans, the caves of the Dordogne in south-west France and the fossil beds of the Siwalik Hills in India furnishing ample proof of this.

Eastward, they crossed from Siberia to Alaska over the isthmus that in those days joined the American and Asiatic continents and which was later cut through, or subsided, to form the present Bering Straits. Traveling east, they scattered over Alaska and finally reached the Atlantic seaboard possibly in the region now covered by the State of New York. South, the remains of mastodon, at least, occur as far down as Patagonia, and the mammoth as far as Mexico. Included in this great distribution—and this takes in both the mammoths and the mastodons—was the territory now known as North Carolina.

In the swamps and morasses of the tide-water section of North Carolina, every opportunity was afforded for an animal to lose its life by bogging down in the peaty soil as domestic cattle do occasionally even to the present day, or at least did before the free-ranges were closed only a few years ago. And, once bogged down, an animal of several tons weight would be very unlikely to escape.

Perhaps some specimens might be caught in mud so soft and deep that the whole animal would, in a very short time, become completely engulfed and sink below the normal water-level, so that the skeleton would remain intact for an almost unlimited period of time—for the fortunate museum collector who happened to discover it.

In other cases death might take place on the surface of the ground, the fleshy parts being eaten by scavenging birds and predacious animals and the bones dragged apart and scattered during the disintegration of the body. Bones remaining on the surface would gradually decompose under the influence of rain, frost and sunshine and completely disappear within a very few years. But such bones as lay on surfaces not sufficiently solid to retain their weight would finally sink below the water-level and there be preserved indefinitely. This below-the-water-level condition was necessary if scientists were ever to secure the remains of extinct animals for investigation and classification, or if museum workers were to add actual parts of prehistoric monsters to their exhibits. Below water-level meant preservation; above water-level meant disintegration.

In the State Museum we have specimens from two species of mammoth and two or three species of mastodon, the latter seeming to have been much more plentiful in eastern North Carolina than the former. Of the mammoths, the two species are represented in one instance by a very perfect molar tooth of six pounds weight, and in the other by a part of a tooth. But even a layman could tell that these two teeth did not come from the same species of animal.

Our most complete mastodon, from Onslow County, is represented by both tusks, all eight of the molar teeth, nearly all of the lower jaw, a part of the upper jaw and a part of the occipital bone. These parts have been assembled and the remainder of the skull roughly modeled, so that we can now show a complete skull of this particular specimen. In addition to the head, we have the three main bones of the right hind leg—femur, tibia and fibula, and the two principal bones of the right fore-leg—humerus and ulna. We also have part of one shoulder-blade, one of the tarsal bones, two ribs, the atlas and a few fragments, which was all we could find of this particular skeleton. The bones of the two legs have now been articulated and mounted, and are shown in an upright case in their proper relationship to each other.

Of another specimen, we have all of the eight molar teeth, part of both tusks and about half a bushel of fragments. We have a number of odd teeth, part of a pelvis, a lower jaw and other fragmentary items representing additional individuals. The above-listed specimens have come from Onslow, Jones, Carteret, Duplin, and New Hanover Counties.

So many other finds of remains of mastodon have come to our knowledge at various times as to make it quite probable that these animals were comparatively numerous in eastern North Carolina in days gone by. Perhaps those were the "Good Old Days" we read about! But I do not think I should care to have lived under the possibility of a herd of mastodons dropping in to eat up all of my garden sass on moonlight nights—in the way that those elephants cleaned up the Martin Johnson's sweet potato patch on Lake Paradise, in east Africa a few years ago.

All fossil remains of animals from the earlier geologic periods are true petrifactions, that is, the animal matter has been replaced by mineral. But in the remains of such comparatively recent forms as the mastodons, the bones have not undergone this change. They are still of true bone tissue, and in drilling the holes necessary in articulating the parts, the drill cuts exactly as if the material were fresh bone. The hollows of the large leg-bones of the Museum mastodon still contained marrow, or at least the adipocere representative of this class of fat. I was sorry afterwards that I did not save some of this marrow for greasing my hunting boots. Too late it occurred to me that hunting boots made waterproof with real mastodon marrow would be unusually good "conjur."

Another point that surprised me very much in working on this specimen was the great difference in the comparative preservation of the molar teeth and the tusks. The former were as hard as flint, the enamel seemingly having not undergone any change, and they were very brittle. The ivory of the tusks, however, had undergone such a change that it had assumed a softness and consistency almost like chalk. In fact, I reinforced the tusks with steel rods for fear that they would not carry their own weight when supported at only one end. Perhaps these mastodon tusks from Onslow County, N. C., are many thousands of years older than most of the mammoth tusks from Siberia, which have a commercial value as ivory, or it may be that the cold-storage conditions under which the Siberian material has come down to us has been a factor in its better preservation.

The future may possibly determine that man inhabited eastern North Carolina along with the mastodons and mammoths, but we have as yet no facts with which to support such a supposition. But it is now generally conceded that man and some of the extinct elephants were co-existent in other parts of North America. Why not in North Carolina?

In the caves of the Dordogne, in France, and in some of the Spanish caves, are found mural drawings and paintings of the mammoth and mastodon that indicate most clearly that the artists knew the animals they reproduced in line and color. As previously stated, no man could imagine an elephant, who had not seen one. The inhabitants of these caves belonged to the Cro-magnon race, which is supposed to have existed some twenty-five to forty thousand years ago, towards the close of the fourth Glacial Period. This race had a great open-air meeting camp at Solutré, in east central France, about which are the remains of many thousands of prehistoric horses, along with the bones of the bison, reindeer and mammoth. Barbecued mammoth must have been quite a dish at these meetings!

The discovery of remains of these extinct elephants is often

—if not usually—accidental. A letter comes to the Museum reporting the discovery of some kind of a horn by a ditch-digger in Jones County. We register interest, suspecting the supposed horn to be a part of the tusk of a mammoth or mastodon. Finally, we secure the specimen, which proves our supposition to be correct. One of us goes down, finds the place of the discovery, and starts digging. The final result of this expedition was part of the other tusk, all of the eight molar teeth, and a lot of fragments; but no large bones. While this work was in progress, we heard of a large bone washed out from the bed of a small stream near Jacksonville, N. C. This clue was followed, and a lot of laborious excavation brought to light the bones previously listed as from Onslow County. All of these were well below the water-level of the stream and most of them below a layer of shell-rock. A cofferdam had to be built around the operation and long, pointed steel rods were used for "sounding." When the rods struck anything that felt like bone, as much water as possible was dipped and pumped out of the cofferdam, and by crawling under water and clawing and hooking around, the bone was usually secured.

In driving down the sheet piling used in building the cofferdam the sharpened plank cut through both tusks. The parts were secured, however, and joined together at the Museum later on.

The best mammoth tooth we have was drawn up by the suction dredge operating in cutting the Inland Waterway between Newport River and Neuse River, and donated to the Museum by the engineer in charge.

We hope someday to secure a complete mastodon skeleton for the Museum, but we have to depend on our friends for information that may lead to the desired end.

PART FIVE

The Lesser Forms of Life: Nature's Smaller Fry

EDITOR'S NOTE

An animal did not need to be as big as a whale to attract the interest of Herbert Brimley, as might be inferred from reading the preceding section. The smaller creatures came in for their share of attention, even though it was usually the bolder, more dashing members of various animal groups, that is, species with strong "personalities," that most appealed to him. Among the smaller animals, birds were easily his favorites. Brimley's contribution to the science of Ornithology consisted of numerous short papers on his observations and collection of North Carolina birds published in "The Auk" and other bird journals as well as his contribution to the two editions of Birds of North Carolina. *That his work was highly regarded is shown by fact that in 1934 he was elected to full membership in the American Ornithologists' Union, and was for a number of years the only resident North Carolinian holding this honor. He especially sought to encourage interest in birds among his layman friends and to "plug" at every opportunity the esthetic value of birds believing that bird study as a hobby could be enjoyed by anyone who had an interest in nature. Thus, birds could be studied from the vantage point of the porch rocker, whereas—well, going after whales or sharks would be an avocation in which few could or would care to indulge!*

Several of Brimley's early articles on birds were included in Parts I and III. The following selections were all written during the last ten years of his life and will serve as samples of those of his articles which were largely written for the bird lover rather than the ornithologist.

Some Aberrant Characteristics
of Birds*

T HE DIFFERENT ORDERS and families of birds are made up of species of similar physical characteristics and, generally speaking, of more or less similar habits. But, at times, one finds a species whose habits diverge materially from those of its near relatives, and it is of certain of these departures from the expected that this paper treats.

Any duck-hunter would tell you that wild ducks in general are noted, among other characteristics, for their alertness to danger and, more particularly, for their speed on the wing, and this is quite true so far as our North American species are concerned. But far to the south of us, along the rocky and stormy shores of the southern part of South America, are found three species of wild duck that can only fly while in contact with the water. They are known as "Steam-boat Ducks," or its Spanish equivalent, and, in flight, the water is beaten into foam by the strokes of their feet and wings. Hence, the name. The largest of these

* Unpublished manuscript.

surface travelers is about the size of a Canada Goose, but I have no information as to their attractiveness as food for man.

In thinking of hawks, in general, particularly of their food, we associate them as preying on various species of birds, mammals, reptiles and insects, many of them using several of the above groups in their diet, and most of them of more than one group. But, the Osprey, or Fish Hawk, feeds on fish exclusively. I believe I am correct in making the statement that all the other fish-catching birds use their bills only in taking their prey, while the Osprey takes its finny prey only with its claws.

Thinking of the Osprey as a true hawk it seems rather strange that this one member of the group should have developed into a diving bird, though in its diving, its feet hit the water ahead of the body, as its claws, and not its bill, constitute its catching equipment, as before indicated.

Prince Rupert's Blue Bird of Paradise might well seek fame for being equipped with the longest English name of any species of bird, but it has another characteristic that seems to be unique among feathered creatures, this being that the male of the species does all of its courting up-side down. Hanging head down from a tree-limb it goes through its courting antics in front of its selected mate and, as the pair finally nests and rears its young, one must suppose that the antics of the male find favor with the coy female.

It would be quite awkward if we humans had to do our courting standing on our heads!

The nesting habits of the Solitary Sandpiper, a fairly common migrant with us, and a not-at-all uncommon species, were unknown until a nest was discovered by Evan Thomson on June 16, 1903. Ornithologists in quest of the nests of this bird had, naturally, looked for them on the ground, this being the nesting habitat of other members of the sandpiper group. The nesting site found by Mr. Thomson, however, was an old Robin's nest and contained 4 eggs of the Sandpiper. Numerous other sets of eggs have since been secured, all of them in old nests of other birds, mostly those of the Robin, but those of the Bronzed Grackle and Canada Jay are also mentioned.

Did any of you ever see a bird fly backwards? You will probably say, no!, at once. But watch a Hummingbird extracting the nectar from a bunch of flowers. Leaving one bloom for another, the Hummer does not turn around in the air in its short flight to the next flower, but backs away, flying backwards to do this, and continuing to face the cluster of blossoms while doing so. A similar action has been noted of an Acadian Flycatcher facing a big bug of some kind in the air, backing away from the bug while continuing to face it.

I had never previously noted the peculiar climbing habits of young American Egrets until visiting the Battery Island Colony near Southport a year or two ago. These particular egrets were in thick Yopon bushes and the young birds did quite a lot of climbing while I was watching them. The climber would reach its wing over a limb above the level of its body and pull itself up until a grip with the other wing, or with the feet, could be taken, and this climbing was not as slow a process as one might imagine. The white feathers on the sides of the bodies and the undersides of wings of all the young ones I saw were badly soiled by dirt and flakes of bark rubbed off the Yopon branches.

There are no doubt good reasons for it but the voluntary captivity of the female Hornbill during the incubation period does seem about as crazy an affair as one could well imagine. Inside a tree-hollow, one selected so that when the bird settles down on its eggs its great bill will project through the opening to the cavity, it allows its mate to build a wall of clay that completely closes the orifice except for an opening around the bill large enough for the play of the bill in receiving food. There the poor female of the species stays, fed daily by its mate, until the eggs are hatched, when the male bird breaks away the wall of clay again to give the said poor female a chance to spread its wings and go a-visiting.

The Man-o'-war-bird is equipped with webbed feet and with a stout hook at the tip of its bill to give it a secure hold of the fish on which it feeds. But it never dives for its food, picking up such fish as it can from the surface, or robbing the gulls and terns that have already captured a fish. No species of bird has a greater command of the air, no fishing bird being able to escape its attacks. Yet its feathers are not waterproof, and if ever it gets down in the water it is unable to rise again and will quickly drown. A very unusual characteristic of a web-footed, fish-eating bird.

The Penguins are another highly specialized group of web-footed birds, the peculiar characteristic in their case being that they do not use their webbed feet in swimming under water, their flipper-like, featherless wings doing all the propelling. This calls for exceptionally developed chest muscles, and such muscles are so developed, and the powerful strokes of the wings so effective that one writer, Dr. Murphy, I think, states that the services of several able-bodied men were required to subdue and tie up an adult Emperor Penguin.

While on the subject of Penguins, two other peculiarities relating to certain members of the group may be mentioned, the first being a wide-spread belief that all species of the group are found only among the icy wastes of the Antarctic. As a matter of fact they stray far from those regions, one species living among the islands of the Galapagos group, which is directly on the Equator.

The other peculiarity is the unusual breeding habits of the Emperor Penguin. This species never sets foot on land but spends its entire life on the ice and in the water, which provide no facilities for nesting. So, when its single egg is laid, it is at once placed on the bird's instep and covered with the warm feathers and a flap of skin belonging to the lower part of the bird's abdomen, where it stays until the chick is hatched. After hatching, the young bird is carried around in the same warm situation as was the egg until it is able to walk on the ice and plunge into the icy waters. Not a very pleasant childhood, one might think.

The Kingfisher group contains individual species that depart in a noticeable degree from habits that we think of as normal to Kingfishers. Our common Belted Kingfisher is just an ordinary Kingfisher except for one departure from the formula. It is the only species of fish-catching bird of which I have knowledge that carries its captive to a perching place and then beats the captured fish on the limb constituting its perch before swallowing it.

Certain of the Asiatic forms of Kingfisher are forest-living birds and feed chiefly on insects, crustaceans, etc., and some of them do not fish at all. The Laughing Jackass—peculiar name for a bird, by the way—is nearly as large as our common crow, but with shorter wings and tail. It is brown in color and feeds mainly on reptiles, insects and crabs. This is an Australian species, its name coming from the supposed resemblance of its cry to that of a jackass. It might, perhaps, be used as a songbird—if one had objectionable neighbors!

The Ruddy Turnstone and the Surf Bird are of the same family but with entirely different nesting habits. Like the Solitary Sandpiper, the Surf Bird's breeding grounds and nesting habits were long unknown, until a pair with a young one was found in the mountains of central Alaska, on June 13, 1921, by O. J. Murie. A nest was discovered in the same region on May 28, 1926. This was the first known nest of the species.

The general habitat of the Surf Bird is the salt-water beaches of the west coast, it moving down as far south as the Straits of Magellan on its fall migration. It is very unusual for a bird of such habits to go back into high mountain country for its period of reproduction. The discoverer of the nest (Joseph Dixon) states that he never found Surf Birds during the nesting period except at elevations of 4,000 feet or more.

The few known nests of the Turnstone have been in high latitudes but in situations such as one might expect to find shore birds, and not among high mountains.

Most wild ducks nest on the ground though a few species use hollow trees for nesting sites, these being the Wood Duck, the Bufflehead, and the two species of Golden-eye. The common Shelduck, or Sheldrake, of Europe and central Asia, seems to be the only member of the Anatidae that nests underground. So far as their nesting habits in England are concerned, they seem to use rabbit burrows, preferably, as nesting sites, the English Rabbit being a burrowing animal.

The Cowbird is a parasite among birds. It neither builds a nest nor cares for its young, laying an egg at a time in the nest of almost any bird of small or medium size that is situated on, or rather near to, the ground. More than a hundred species of birds in the United States have been recorded as so victimized. The sexes do not pair, the habits of both being promiscuous, so they have no family cares of any kind. The most objectionable part of the parasitic habits of this bird is that the laying of the egg among other eggs of the builder and owner of the nest is usually a death-warrant for the young of the nest's owner. The young Cowbird is a bully and manages to secure most of the food brought in to feed the whole brood, at the expense of the other occupants of the nest.

The Hoatzin is a primitive bird of South America that, in the young, is provided with hooked claws on the thumb and index finger bones of each wing to enable it to climb from the water up to the limb on which its home nest is situated, and any other climbing that may be necessary. It is a leaf-eater. It is only the young birds that are able to swim and dive.

In the case of the true ostriches, the two species that inhabit Africa and southwest Asia, the toe formula is reduced to two, the hind-toe and the second toe being missing, the only species of bird that are two-toed, I believe. The South American Ostriches, or Rheas, have three toes.

The terns in general are usually considered as fish-eaters but two species of tern feed partly on insects, caught in the air. Bent * says that in the interior of the country the Black Tern is entirely insectivorous, but Brewster says that off the coast of Massachusetts they also feed on fish. In my experience with the species on the North Carolina coast I have never seen one fishing but have frequently seen them catching insects on the wing. The Roseate Tern seems to be much more of a fish-eater than is the Black Tern, but I have seen them catching insects while flying, on Pea Island, and other observers report the same habit.

While talking of terns it might be in order to mention the Fairy Tern of the Southern Hemisphere, particularly a peculiarity in its nesting habits. According to those familiar with the

* *Life Histories of North American Gulls and Terns,* Bulletin 113, U. S. Nat. Mus.

e Snowy Egret. This species has plumes on both back and head during the breed-
; season. Shown also is a Louisiana Heron. (*Allan D. Cruickshank from National
dubon Society*)

e American Egret has plumes only on the back. Note the long plumes on the birds
the extreme right and left. Near the center is a Snowy Egret with head plumes
d dark bill. (*Allan D. Cruickshank from National Audubon Society*)

Above, Ruby-throated Hummingbird female on her nest which is a masterpiece bird architecture blending perfectly with its surroundings. *Below,* The Kingfisher familiar fisherman along streams and on lakes. Since it takes small fish only, it not a competitor with human fishermen. (*Both, Allan D. Cruickshank from Natio Audubon Society*)

bird in its natural haunts it must be one of the most beautiful of birds. Its immaculate plumage, accentuated by a dark ring around the eye, seem to give it an almost transparent appearance when seen against the sky, but the nesting feature above-mentioned is that it not only chooses a bare projection of rock for a depository of its single egg, but frequently lays it in an almost indistinguishable depression on the upper side of a comparatively small tree limb. I have seen photographs of the egg of a Fairy Tern so placed that it looked as if the mere alighting of its owner on the same limb might cause the egg to roll off. How in the world the Tern can cover the egg, and leave it, without its falling off the limb is difficult to understand.

Going away from home a few thousand miles we find what is perhaps the most peculiar breeding habit among all birds in the Brush Turkey of the Australasian region. This bird seems to have no fixed nesting period and no home cares. When the hen turkey feels like it she throws dirt backwards with her feet until quite a pile has accumulated, circling around the growing mound while doing this. In this pile she digs a hole a foot or more deep, lays an egg in the hole, covers it up, and goes off on unfinished business leaving the egg to hatch by heat of sun. Other turkey hens find the pile, add material to it, lay each an egg, and leave for parts unknown. This goes on year after year until a community pile of dirt has accumulated that may measure many feet in diameter and several feet deep. One such "nest" is reported as having a height of eight feet and a circumference of sixty feet.

Any time a Brush Turkey hen feels like contributing another name to the census she visits the sand-hill and lays another egg.

The young bird comes out of the shell fully feathered and is able to fly within an hour. It burrows out of the dirt, shakes the loose particles from its feathers, and goes out into the world to seek its fortune. It knows no parents, as its parents know no offspring. A sort of congenital orphan, as it were.

Unusual Actions of a Phoebe[*]

O~N~ N~OVEMBER~ 27 I was on a deer stand in Onslow County, N. C. The air was rather warm for the time of year and mosquitoes were quite noticeably in evidence though not particularly aggressive. I was in a standing position with my rifle under my arm, the barrel pointing downward, and I had my hands clasped in front. A faint fluttering of wings caused me to look down, and I saw a Phoebe (*Sayornis phoebe*), a bird frequently known by us as Winter Pewee, trying to alight on my rifle barrel. Failing to secure a firm grip on the smooth surface of the metal, the bird slid down the barrel until the front sight was reached, where it secured the grip desired, and there it perched.

It showed no sign of fear or nervousness and in a few seconds flew up and picked a mosquito off my hands, which were not more than a foot distant from its perch. Then, it picked others

* *The Auk*, LI (April, 1934), 237-38.

off the front of my coat, off my sleeves, and several more off my hands, meanwhile perching indiscriminately on my hands, sleeves, and gun barrel, though seeming to prefer the last.

Finally, the Phoebe discovered that my face seemed to be attracting more mosquitoes than any other part of my person so he transferred his attention to that part of my anatomy, and found a new perching place on the top of my hunting cap.

In picking mosquitoes off my face, the sharp points of the bird's bill were noticeably felt at every capture, and it was the irritation caused by a succession of these pricks that finally caused me to dispense with its attentions. Mosquitoes were also taken by the bird off the back of my neck and my left ear, but none from the right ear.

I counted twenty times that the Phoebe perched on my rifle and twenty catches of mosquitoes taken off my face, and then stopped counting. I estimated that the number of separate perchings on the gun barrel reached at least forty, the mosquitoes taken off my face between thirty-five and forty, and that the total number of those insects taken off my person numbered sixty or seventy altogether.

When I decided to end the incident, I found a difficulty in doing so. I had presumed that any decided movement on my part would drive my little friend away, but this bird was not of the scary kind. He had learned that I was the community center for mosquitoes in that immediate vicinity, and evidently recognized and appreciated a good eating place when he found one. So he continued to perch on my head and pick mosquitoes off my face even after I had started to move around in an effort to discourage his attentions. But my face was beginning to feel somewhat inflamed from the frequent pecking to which it had been subjected, so I called it a day and told the Phoebe to stop pestering me.

Several times during the Phoebe's visit, it would, after taking a mosquito off my person, perch on a dead branch of a six-foot pine sapling about four feet distant from where I was standing. Once, while it was occupying this branch, I slowly stretched out my arm towards it, with the fore-finger extended to within about one foot of its perch, and it immediately foresook the latter for my finger.

Two days later, a man occupying a stand about a hundred and fifty yards distant from where the above-described incidents occurred, related that a small bird had approached him, perched on various parts of his body, and every now and then fluttered directly in front of his face. But that morning was cold, with no mosquitoes in evidence.

Subsequent to this, three other deer hunters occupying the same or near-by stands reported intimate visits from a small, dull-colored bird, and it would seem to be fairly safe to presume that it was the same individual Phoebe in all five cases.

The above took place in a wild section of the lower part of Onslow County, North Carolina, with no residence or cleared land near by. It is quite possible that this individual Phoebe had never seen a human before and, finding that the object around which the mosquitoes collected was no more dangerous than any other stump in the woods, even if it did possess the power of movement, mentally included me as just one more object properly belonging in the landscape.

My outer dress on that morning was khaki-colored cap and coat and dark corduroy breeches.

I Like Blue Jays!*

I KNOW THAT I am sticking out my neck in making the statement that I like to have Blue Jays around my home.

Roger Tory Peterson's beautiful colored pictures of this bird, together with some notes not unfavorable to its habits, that appeared in the June first issue of *Life* magazine, brought forth several rather severe criticisms of the nice things the article had said about the species. One lady critic writing as follows: "Last Tuesday I was innocently standing in the yard when I received a severe whack on the back of my head. It was a Blue Jay that delivered the blow."

Now wasn't that too bad, even for a ferocious Blue Jay? But I trust that the bird's victim is by this time convalescing nicely and on the high road to a complete recovery. Most of the writers, however, confined their criticisms to the egg-eating and supposedly quarrelsome habit of the bird—which is the line usually

* *The Chat*, VI, No. 5 (November, 1942), 70-71.

followed in this connection—the critics losing sight of the fact that in all of its activities it is merely acting as a Blue Jay.

The species that nest fairly regularly on my lot and those adjacent thereto are Blue Jay, Catbird, Cardinal, Brown Thrasher, Robin and Wood Thrush, with Yellow-throated Vireo, Chipping Sparrow, Summer Tanager and Ruby-throated Hummingbird occurring at rare intervals. So far as I can determine, after occupying the same house for thirty-two years, the summer population of the six commonly observed species varies but little from year to year. Only one pair of jays seems to breed in the immediate vicinity, with often more than a single pair of the other five on hand nearly every year.

But to get back to our Blue Jays! A most pleasing picture to the eye—at least to my eyes—and even more in evidence when the leaves are off the trees and bird life comparatively scarce. A family party of four or five Blue Jays, acting among the bare branches of the oaks, is a most welcome and attractive picture, and I would much rather they would eat a few eggs of other birds in the summer than fail in their most welcome presence in the winter.

On the terrace in front of my home is a very lovely little willow oak, some seven or eight years old, a volunteer tree. Others have come up around the lot, with no acorn-bearing trees of this species near enough in any direction to account for the presence of willow oak acorns unless brought there by the jays. To my mind, the presence of that beautiful little oak on the terrace makes amends for many a sucked egg of Catbird, Robin, Wood Thrush, or Brown Thrasher.

There is no inferiority complex about the Blue Jay. It usually seems to know what it wants, and to go after it, which really might be regarded as a commendable characteristic. Self-assertive? Yes, decidedly so; and why not? It would seem rather monotonous if all our feathered friends were shy, shrinking creatures; a little mixture of pugnacity helps to leaven the whole.

When the great liner, the Queen Mary, was on her maiden trip across the Atlantic some of the newspaper correspondents aboard started criticizing certain details of the ship in comparison with corresponding features of the Italian "Rex," the French "Normandie," and the German "Bremen." A more broadminded member of the guild shut off the critics rather cleverly with the following statement: "True, the Queen Mary is not the Rex, nor is she the Bremen, nor the Normandie. She is Sandy's idea of a ship—and Sandy had been building ships for a *long, long* time."

So, the Blue Jay is one of nature's ideas of a bird, and nature has been developing birds even longer than is generally implied by "a long, long time."

*Hawks**

I<small>N SPITE OF THE</small> animosity towards hawks as a whole that is characteristic of many farmers and sportsmen, it is a group of birds that has always had an appeal to me that has caused me to overlook the objectionable features that really do belong to some species.

Quite recently, the writer was idly scanning the pages of a book published in Philadelphia in 1819. The author of the book was a Doctor David Ramsay, and the rather fulsome title of the work is as follows: "Universal History Americanized, an Historical View of the World, from the Earliest Records to the Year 1808." This book was Vol. VII (out of twelve, in all) and I there found the statement that the principal exports of Iceland consisted chiefly of dried fish, salmon, brimstone, eider-down and falcons. Possibly the only record of a species of hawk being listed among the major exports of any country. It was certainly news to me.

* Unpublished manuscript written about 1940.

Above, Phoebe, the friendly flycatcher which often builds its nest under bridges or porches. A phoebe persisted in perching on Mr. Brimley's gunbarrel. *Below*, The Blue Jay, though generally unpopular, has some redeeming features. Among other things, it helps in reforestation by planting nuts and seeds. (*Both, Allan D. Cruickshank from National Audubon Society*)

Red-tailed Hawk, one of the large soaring hawks, often miscalled "Hen hawk." (*Karl H. Maslowski from National Audubon Society*)

Sparrowhawk, a small, gentle falco which feeds largely on insects and mic (*Paul J. Fair from National Audubo Society*)

The Nighthawk or Bullbat below is protecting its egg, shown on the gravel in th foreground. No nest is made or needed as the egg resembles rocks of a similar shape These birds often lay their eggs on gravel roofs in cities. This useful bird feeds onl on flying insects. (*John H. Gerard from National Audubon Society*)

Of course these falcons were shipped alive, the species almost to a certainty being one of the forms known as gyrfalcons, the largest of any of the long-winged hawk group formerly used in the sport of falconry. These gyrfalcons are birds of the north.

The hawks, eagles, and kites all belong to the same family, the eagles constituting a group that has reached the gigantic in size compared with the other members of the family and, by reason of the superior size and power of its members, such have established a name for ferocity, nobility and fearlessness that is not always borne out by facts.

The bald eagle, for instance, does not spend most of its time in screaming for liberty, trying to stare the sun out of countenance and in robbing the farmer of his pigs and lambs. It is much more likely to be found robbing the fish hawk of its hardearned prey or sailing along the ocean beach or the shores of sound or river looking for a dead fish left by the angler or commercial fisherman. It is particularly partial to a fish diet and a putrid specimen seems to be just as acceptable as a perfectly fresh fish stolen from an osprey.

I once flushed a bald eagle from the carcass of an alligator that I had killed and skinned a day or two earlier, the eagle feasting on the smelly alligator meat in company with several turkey vultures. And that eagle as it left its meal was attacked by a weak little kingbird that literally ran the king of birds out of the country. The kingbird attacking the king of birds indicated that the former had not been misnamed, though the latter might have been.

During the duck-shooting season, the bald eagle makes a percentage of its living off crippled ducks, wounded but not secured by the sportsmen.

The golden eagle may also feed on carrion but generally speaking, it is a cleaner feeder than its relative. The stomach of one received at the museum a few years ago contained the remains of a goat kid. But this is very much the rarer of the two species found in North Carolina and the probability is that 90 per cent of the eagles seen in the state belong to the first-mentioned species.

Of a number of specimens of both species of eagle that have passed through the hands of the workers at the State Museum the following data regarding their maximum size have been gathered: golden eagle, greatest expanse of extended wing, 7 feet, heaviest specimen 11 pounds; bald eagle, greatest wing expanse 7 feet 3 inches, maximum weight 10½ pounds.

It may be well to note here that in all the species of the hawk family that occur in North Carolina the female is a larger and more powerful bird than the male, in some cases the difference in the size of the sexes being quite pronounced. An experiencd observer can frequently determine the sex of a specimen at a glance.

Only two species of the group known as kites have been recorded from this State, the swallow-tailed kite and the Mississippi kite, and both species are among our rarest hawks. The Mississippi kite is a very rare straggler having been recorded only twice, in 1903 and 1907, both times from Cherokee County.

The swallow-tailed kite has been seen by the writer on several occasions, but only in the region of Lake Ellis, in Craven County. While quite rare, it was known to many of the local people, "Snake Hawk" being the name by which it was locally known. With its pure white head and underparts contrasting sharply with the solid black of the back, and a long, deeply-forked tail, it is a bird of most striking appearance, its graceful flight being an added feature of attractiveness.

The swallow-tail has also been recorded from Black Mountain and Lake Waccamaw and while it seems to be a rare summer visitor with us it has not been recorded as a nesting species in North Carolina. Both of these species of kite feed mainly on small reptiles and on some of the larger insects.

Three species of the group known as Buteos with us, and as buzzards in European countries, occur in this State, the red-tailed hawk and the red-shouldered hawk being with us among the commonest species in the whole family. The red-tailed species is one of our largest hawks, being a heavy, powerfully built bird whose size and impressiveness tend to make the uninformed observer give it credit for destructiveness that it does not deserve.

These two Buteos feed mainly on field rats and mice, lizards, small snakes and insects. The red-tail does kill a chicken at times and an occasional wild bird, but the red-shouldered hawk is one of the greatest destroyers of rats and mice that we have.

The third member of this group, the broad-winged hawk, is a much smaller bird and follows its larger relatives in its avoidance of taking feathered prey. The broad-wing is not a resident with us, going south for the winter.

But when we reach the so-called big and little "blue darters" we are among a group that mainly selects its food from among the feathered population of our woods and fields.

The largest and fiercest of this group is the goshawk, a northern species that has not been reported as occurring in this state. The two blue darters above referred to are the Cooper's hawk and the sharp-shinned hawk, both species more or less common with us, the larger of the two, the Cooper's hawk, is probably responsible for the destruction of more of the farmer's chickens than all other native hawks combined. It is also partial to ground-nesting game birds, such as quail and ruffed grouse. A family group of Cooper's hawk, including adult and young birds in the nest is on display in the Museum.

The sharp-shinned hawk, a smaller and therefore weaker, bird, necessarily prefers smaller birds for its nourishment. But my brother, C. S. Brimley, once killed a sharp-shin that had caught a flicker, a bird heavier than itself.

The marsh hawk is placed in a genus to itself though other closely-related species, the hen harrier, for instance, are found in European countries. This hawk can always be readily identified in flight by the large white spot above the base of the tail. It is the only species of our native hawks that nests on the ground, a rather natural nesting site for a species that is hardly ever seen in woods but most frequently seen quartering the ground over meadow, marsh or open field. This bird hunts mainly for rats and mice but a percentage of small birds of the open ground form a part of its daily fare.

Before the development of fire-arms to the point where the successful killing of game birds in flight was practicable, the recognized methods of taking birds was almost confined to netting, bird-liming and hawking, the latter being the true sporting method of taking feathered game. As the care of the hawks called for the employment of specialists (the "falconer" being a recognized official in a well-ordered household), and hawks being of considerable monetary value, the sport of falconry was necessarily confined to the nobility and gentry of the various countries in which this phase of taking game was customary.

This sport had its own glossary of terms, most of which are now obsolete, and the male and female of the various species of falcon that were used were allotted different names.

The only species of falcon found in North Carolina are the duck hawk, pigeon hawk and sparrow hawk. The first of these is the American representative of the peregrine falcon of Europe, the peregrine being among the choicest of the hawks used by the old-time falconers. Anatomically, the falcons are distinguished from other hawks by the presence of a tooth on the edge of the upper mandible with a notch between that and the tip of the beak, but, practically, by their ardor in the chase of other birds, their superior powers of flight and in their susceptibility to training.

One species other than the falcons was used in hawking, this being the goshawk previously mentioned. The goshawk fastens to its prey when it strikes it in the air and carries it to the ground, or to a perch, for the feast that follows. The falcon, at least the larger species, kills its feathered prey in the air by a lightning-like strike allowing it to fall to earth as the falcon follows it down for its meal. This is the usual procedure but if the game caught is small enough to be carried easily the falcon may kill and carry after the manner of the goshawk group. This latter belonged to what the falconers called "short-winged" hawks, the swifter falcons going under the name of "long-winged" hawks.

Our native duck hawk is regarded by the experts as the swiftest bird that flies. Its speed and command of the air are so well described by another writer that I am quoting the statement in question. Forbush in his *Birds of Massachusetts* gives a description of the flight of this bird, by Chamberlain, as follows: "Its flight is one of the most wonderful exhibitions of speed and command of the air shown by any bird. At times when heading into the wind it will slide off sidewise covering a mile thus in the matter of seconds. It can so regulate its flight at will as seemingly to bound upward for one hundred or two hundred feet like a flash and apparently with the greatest of ease. It can overtake and capture any of our birds in flight except possibly the chimney swift, and the only hope its victims have to elude it is by dodging its rushes until they can dive into some tangle of vine and shrubbery."

We became very fond of the pet sparrow hawk we kept in the Museum some years ago. It was secured as a young bird and was never in a cage. It had the free run of our offices and work-rooms and often left these rooms for exploratory trips through the exhibit halls. It would perch on our shoulders and heads and sometimes on the frame of a typewriter while the machine was in use. But it developed an unfortunate habit of perching on the wire guard of an electric fan and, on one occasion while doing this, it allowed one of its feet to come in contact with the revolving blades, from which it suffered a broken leg. But Harry Davis expertly set the fracture, using splints, and in about a couple of weeks the leg was as good as ever.

One day, while I was talking to a small group of visitors in the Museum, one of whom was a girl wearing a dark-colored dress with red trimmings, the sparrow hawk appeared out of nowhere, took a firm grip on the girl's dress with its sharp claws and began pecking at a red bow, evidently associating the color with the red meat on which it was accustomed to being fed. It was quite an experience for the girl.

But our pet came to a tragic end, once it had found its way out of doors. The first time this occurred it was caught on Halifax Street and returned to us by some Boy Scouts who recognized it as a Museum pet. The following morning, on opening the office door, our little hawk made a straight flight through the Museum from the Salisbury Street side of the building to freedom on Halifax Street. We sent out an alarm, but with no results. But late that afternoon a janitor from the Capitol brought us a badly injured sparrow hawk with the following story of its capture. The janitor was cleaning up the Senate Chamber, with all windows open. Suddenly, he observed a ferocious bird flying directly at him. Assuming an attitude of defense, he beat the bird down with his trusty broom as soon as it came within range and was much surprised—and perhaps rather humiliated—to learn that it was merely a tame bird approaching him in a friendly attitude to perch on his shoulders, and not a wild man-eating hawk.

PART SIX

The North Carolina State Museum: A Lasting Memorial to H. H. Brimley

EDITOR'S NOTE

As we have indicated in the opening pages of this volume the State Museum was Brimley's life work and great love; it remains today as a lasting memorial.. Something of the history of the museum is sketched in the first two articles in this section. During the early years a strong emphasis was placed on agricultural exhibits since the museum was set up as a division of the State Department of Agriculture. As the function of agricultural education was gradually taken over by other agencies, geology and natural history became more and more the central theme of the exhibits and educational work. It is doubtful if the average museum visitor fully appreciates the skill and hard work necessary for the preparation of a good exhibit; reading the last two articles will leave no doubts on this score. The accomplishments of Brimley and his staff are remarkable when one considers that his operating budget was relatively small and he often lacked materials and aids which would be considered routine in a large city museum. The last article, depicting the solution of the many problems connected with preparation of a huge whale skeleton, is a fitting climax to this volume. The title of this paper, "Do What You Can Now With What You Have," might well be taken to represent Mr. Brimley's philosophy of life. It can be truthfully said that he did a lot with what he had!

The State Museum in 1915[*]

T he State Museum is an institution designed to educate the visitor in the natural resources and natural history of the State. The first of these divisions covers the agricultural and horticultural products, the timber and mineral wealth, the commercial fisheries, and the game birds and animals. The latter takes cognizance of all bird, animal, fish, reptile and other life of the State.

As the Museum is a division of the State Department of Agriculture, a good deal of the efforts of the force in charge has latterly been along the lines of agricultural education. Models have been prepared in the Museum work rooms illustrating the various methods used in the planting of fruit trees; well planted and properly cared for orchards are shown alongside of others of the opposite character. A tenth-acre tomato patch, with the vines of various dates of planting in place, is exhibited, to illustrate the teachings of the Girls Canning Clubs work. All these

[*] Published in the *Charlotte Daily Observer,* February 17, 1915.

are made to scale, so that the visitor can absorb at a glance the main features of the lessons presented.

One of the finest and most complete collections of grains and grasses that the writer has ever seen outside an exposition was made last summer when a North Carolina exhibit at the San Francisco Exposition this year seemed a possibility. When the exposition idea fell through, this collection was installed in the Museum, and here it remains as an object lesson of our agricultural products and possibilities. Each sheaf of grain, so far as it has been possible to carry out the plan, is accompanied by a glass jar containing a sample of the cleaned grain produced from the same crop, and all are labelled with the name of the variety and the name and address of the grower. A bundle of rye, with many of the stalks more than seven feet in length, is noticeable in this collection. This was grown on the Department's Buncombe county Test Farm.

Fruits in glass, and a very complete collection of pecans and native nuts are features of interest, and specimens of the goods put up by the Tomato Club girls again call attention to the great educational work the Agricultural Department is carrying on among our country girls and boys.

An exhibit of model farm barns, silos, cow stalls, and other farm buildings and appliances is under consideration, as well as an exhibit of mounted specimens of the best varieties of live stock for the farmer to breed. All these take time in working up, however, and progress along these lines is slower than one could wish.

A large series of colored photographs of farming scenes and activities decorates the walls of the Agricultural Room.

It is doubtful if any State in the Union produces a greater variety of valuable stones than are shown here as products of North Carolina. The widely-known Mt. Airy granite, the pink Rowan county granite, a white marble from Mitchell county, the blue-gray Cherokee county marbles, and a great variety of sandstones, are only a few of the many that the Museum exhibits in the form of polished spheres, turned columns, and cut cubes.

Orbicular diorite, from Davie county, and the oddly marked leopardite, from Mecklenburg county, are two unique types of ornamental stone.

Gold ores, iron ores, copper ores, are exhibited in great profusion, and limestone, talc, mica (of which North Carolina is the largest producer among the States), kaolin (china clay), chromite, manganese, monazite (used in the production of incandescent gas mantles), barytes, and many other minerals of economic value are also shown. And, while practically none of the State's kaolin is burned within our borders, a case of handsome china-ware is exhibited as a product of our white clays—manufactured in East Liverpool, Ohio, and Trenton, New Jersey!

There is a very attractive case of native gem stones, both cut and in the rough, some of the specimens being particularly well-colored, of great brilliance, and valuable. Rhodolite—a strictly North Carolina gem—other garnets, golden beryl, blue beryl, aquamarine, emerald, rose quartz, carnelian, crystal quartz, amethyst, smoky "topaz," catseye corundum, ruby corundum, sagenite, and hiddenite, are among those shown.

In the same case are several specimens of meteorite. Did you ever stop to think that meteorites are the only known communication we have with other worlds—and that they all come one way? Curiously enough—or quite naturally, as one views the matter—these, falling from the vast expanses of the ether beyond our Earth's atmosphere, are mainly composed of elements that are the same as this world's crust. Iron, a common constituent of meteorites, is an example of this.

One of the meteorites exhibited in the Museum—that from Rich Mountain, in Jackson county—was seen to fall at two o'clock in the afternoon, June 20, 1903. This is very unusual, and adds interest to the specimen.

Several very large fish hanging on the wall—tarpon, shark, sting ray, sturgeon, etc.,—tell the visitor that he has entered the "Fisheries" Room. Here, the cases contain mounted specimens of all our more important food and game fishes, and along with them are shown the lines, hooks, nets, etc., with which the fish are caught. On the walls are pictures of the various phases of the great seine fisheries of the Albemarle Sound, of oystering, mullet seining, purse netting, etc. An eight hundred pound leatherback turtle is a revelation to the man from up-country, and a thirty pound snapping turtle is another object of interest rather than of beauty.

Talking of snakes, perhaps the big mounted diamond-backed rattler, six feet long, with a head three inches across, and which weighed eight pounds before skinning, is about as dangerous a reptile as one would wish to meet. This comes from Craven county, as did the nine foot alligator on the wall. A much larger alligator is in the Museum work rooms, where a group of marsh-loving reptiles is in course of preparation.

In the downstairs Forestry Rooms is exhibited one of the most complete collections of native timbers shown by any State. Some curly poplar planks, of large size and highly finished, call attention to the possibilities of this most beautiful wood, and a yellow poplar plank, five and a half feet wide, gives an idea of the size to which this magnificent tree grows. Sections of the same kind of tree six feet in diameter emphasize this point. But perhaps the most remarkable timber specimen of all is a cross section of a cypress, cut twenty feet above the ground, that measures five feet in smallest diameter! When this great disc is thoroughly seasoned it will be cut through and one of the faces will be finished and polished to bring out the grain and the annual rings. A more or less incomplete counting of the rings gives the age of this tree as being somewhere between eight hundred and fifty and nine hundred years! The growth of this forest monarch was so slow that at certain periods of its life, a couple of centuries or so ago, it required about eighty-six years to add two inches to its diameter! And it was growing in a swamp near Kinston when William the Conqueror invaded England in 1066! The stump of this great tree measured eleven feet one inch across, four feet above the ground level, when it was finally cut down in the fall of 1913.

Black birch, wild cherry, curly ash, black walnut, sycamore, quartered white oak, curly maple, etc., show what the State possesses in beautiful cabinet woods, while the woods of wider use in all sorts of structural work are not neglected.

A few curiosities, such as a brick embedded deep in the wood of a growing tree, and found by the saw (!), pine bark eight inches thick, freak growths, etc., are exhibited along with such objects of minor economic importance as "briar" pipe stock, turned wooden bowls (some of them large enough for bath tubs), baskets, bread plates, and a cone built up of twenty-two different kinds of North Carolina woods.

Many more visitors find interest in the natural history side of a museum than in any other of its departments, and we have a State that is abundantly supplied with material for satisfying this interest.

Hanging overhead in the first Zoological Room is the great whale skeleton that was originally the framework of an animal fifty feet long and weighing well along towards a hundred tons. A large case contains twenty-two species of wild ducks, four of wild geese, and one of wild swan, all native to our great sounds and marshes. A family group of deer, others of possums, skunk, ground·hogs, wild cats, etc., call attention to the life-histories of a few of our more valuable game and fur-bearing animals. Several cases contain specimens, with their nests and eggs, of our insect-eating birds, without which the farmer and fruit grower would have a much harder job than he has now in maturing his crops. One large case calls attention to the bird life of a typical marsh in the central portion of the State, while another shows the two species of eagle that respectively inhabit our mountains and the seashore—in all their stages of plumage.

The second Zoological Room, having too little direct daylight to show up any exhibits satisfactorily, has been divided up into series of cases lighted artificially, and in these are installed more groups of birds and animals of economic importance or of general interest. The two species of egret—those birds of the beautiful plumes that have caused their downfall almost to the point of extinction—are shown with nests, eggs and young, all the specimens coming from the only place in the State where they still exist, on the strictly protected lands and waters of Mr. James

Sprunt, of Wilmington, who most kindly allowed the collection and permanent preservation of these most beautiful creatures while there was yet time.

Our greatest game bird, the wild turkey, is represented by two magnificent gobblers; and another large bird, though hardly game, is shown feeding on the carcass of a hog that had died from hog cholera, that bane of the pork raiser. The lesson taught by this latter case, and emphasized by the label, is that all "cholera carcasses" should be burned or buried, to prevent the spread of this dread disease by buzzards, worthless dogs, and other similar agents. This particular group attracted much attention at the National Corn Exposition, at Columbia, two years ago.

The above is a brief sketch of a few of the features found in our State Museum, enough, perhaps, to induce the reader unfamiliar with the place to pay it a visit when opportunity occurs. Do not think that we are neglected now, however, as we have in the neighborhood of a hundred thousand visitors a year. On Thursday of State Fair Week in 1913, something over eight thousand *counted* visitors entered the Museum doors, and more than four thousand came in the day previous. Raleigh will average fifty out-of-town excursions during the summer and on many days during the year from five hundred to a thousand people go through the Museum rooms. Every school and college in Raleigh, as well as others from out of town, uses the place for classes—including even the Institution for the Blind! We make a practice of opening some of the cases and allowing the blind children to handle certain specimens under supervision, and it is most interesting, though at times rather pitiful, to hear the exclamations of a little blind child "seeing" a deer, or a bear, or a fox for the first time. It is wonderful, too, to note what knowledge of form and texture the extra-sensitive fingertips of a blind person convey to his brain.

The State Museum in 1928*

In 1851, the General Assembly of North Carolina provided for the establishment of the office of State Geologist. Among the duties of this office was that of making and keeping a collection of the rocks and minerals of the State, and the collections so made formed the nucleus of the present State Museum.

Later, the State Geologist was placed under the direction and supervision of the Department of Agriculture, and it followed that the afore-mentioned collections came under the control of this Department along with the office. And the Museum has remained a division of the Department of Agriculture from that day to the present time.

At a still later date, the scope of the Museum was extended to include collections of objects illustrating "the Agricultural and the Natural History and the Natural Resources of the State."

* Condensed from an article originally prepared for the *Raleigh Times*, January 11, 1929.

This limitation of the Museum's activities—both geographically and by subjects—has been decidedly beneficial in preventing any attempt to cover too much ground, a common failing in many of the smaller and medium-sized museums, as such attempts usually result in a multiplicity of subjects being included, with the result that many of them are covered too thinly to be of any service to the public.

STATE-WIDE APPEAL

With the above limitations, the Museum has a State-wide appeal to the citizenship of North Carolina, including a definite contribution to the educational and recreational needs of the people at large. Outside of the State, it is also well known, its value in advertising the Natural Resources and other features of the State being widely recognized.

The word "growth," as applied to a museum, may have various meanings. In the physical kind—that relating to an increase in the floor space occupied—there is nothing to report in the past three years, but in other kinds of growth progress can be shown.

A growth in character has undoubtedly taken place. By this is meant more attractive exhibition rooms, a closer attention to cleanliness, improvements in the installation of exhibits, improved lighting in some of the rooms and other factors tending to add to the appeal of the institution as a whole to those who make use of it.

ACTIVITIES EXPAND

A new practice has been adopted, that of donating small but representative collections of minerals to the science departments of various educational institutions of the State that have made applications therefor. Another addition to the activities of the members of the Museum force is that of making addresses before civic clubs, science clubs and other bodies on matters connected with the work of the Museum. A number of such addresses have been made and, during the past year, three radio talks have also been made.

The growth of the Museum's appeal to the public on all counts is best indicated by the increase in attendance figures. During the calendar year 1926, the number of visitors amounted to 112,-434. In 1927, the total was 142,774, and the first eleven months of 1928 show a total of 164,009, the latter figures indicating a total attendance for 1928 of well over 175,000. There are two features connected with these attendance figures that are worthy of mention, the first being that the number of visitors attending the Museum annually is more than four times the population of the city in which it is situated. This is unique among the museums of the United States so far as information is available. The second feature is the low cost of operation per visitor. Definite figures from only a few other museums are available in this connection, but others can be estimated, and the result shows at least that this institution operates on a basis of very close economy.

The fact that somewhere about three hundred group classes from the schools and colleges of the State visit the Museum annually is a further indication of its value as a medium for visual education. These classes come from a radius of more than 150 miles from Raleigh, the maximum distance being about 170 miles.

Last spring a group of senior and graduate students from McPherson College, Kansas, spent a whole day in the Museum, asking questions, examining the exhibits and taking notes. As they were leaving, the director of the party, Professor H. H. Nininger, of the McPherson College Faculty, stated that this North Carolina institution was one of the three museums his party had visited in the seven months it had been on the road, that seemed to be doing really constructive work. And his party was making this nine months automobile trip, covering the whole of the collegiate year, with the express purpose of visiting all the museums it could reach within the time at its disposal. The Pacific Coast had been visited, taking in all the museums between Kansas and California on the way, and the trip back to Kansas was by way of the Southern tier of States to Florida and thence back home by way of the Eastern Seaboard and the Northern New England and mid-Western States. The above-mentioned statement by Professor Nininger was, perhaps, the highest compliment ever paid the North Carolina State Museum by an individual so particularly qualified to judge.

OPEN EVERY WEEK DAY

In connection with the matter of attendance, it may be noted that the Museum is open to the public for the whole day on every day in the year except Sundays and Christmas Day, and, during the summer months, when other State departments close at 4:30 p.m., the Museum is kept open until 5:30.

The notable accessions to the collections show up very favorably for the biennium, more so than for any like period in the past. Of course, the big bull Sperm Whale, fifty-five feet in length, is the one outstanding specimen, both as to size and as to comparative rarity, that has ever come to the Museum. There may also be mentioned the large Ocean Sunfish, from Swansboro, estimated to weigh between 1200 and 1300 pounds; an eleven and a half foot alligator, a sail fish, an octopus with a five-foot spread of arms; a sixteen-foot Thresher Shark, from Wilmington; a very large Red Drum from Ocracoke, a yellow Raccoon, a pure Albino Opossum, a large specimen of Black Bear and a number of specimens of rare birds.

The Thresher Shark above referred to measures about seven and a half feet for head and body and has about eight and a half feet of tail, and it is the first record of this species on the North Carolina coast, or at least the first specimen known to have been secured. It was caught near Wilmington in November of last year.

GIANT OF EXHIBITS

The skeleton of the Sperm Whale is larger than that of the Right Whale already on exhibition in the Museum. Besides its greater size, it will be noticeable for the differences in its structure, particularly in the skull. The skull differences are so great that one would hardly recognize relationship between the two as belonging to the same group of animals.

Several hundred geological specimens have been added to the collections during the period as well as a large number in zoology. A collection of native pottery has also been secured from several of the firms and individuals now engaged in this comparatively new line of work. All these, of course, are manufactured from native clays. In both geology and zoology, however, the exhibits are far from complete and there is a lot of work ahead before either group will be anything like fully representative. Other duties have prevented any systematic collecting work during the four years under discussion, and collecting trips are absolutely necessary in filling the many gaps.

The large cypress disc from Lenoir County has been finished and placed on exhibition. This disc was cut twenty feet above the ground and measures about five and a half feet in diameter. The tree from which it came was about 840 years old when cut in 1913, and the stump measured eleven feet one inch in diameter four feet above the ground.

AGRICULTURAL EXHIBIT

Additional material for the agricultural exhibit was secured from the recent State Fair, but the exhibit is still incomplete. Next harvest season, however, it is hoped that many additions can be made.

The original twenty-four water-color paintings from which the color plates in the volume on the birds of North Carolina were made, were presented to the Museum by the State Audubon Society in 1925. And a very interesting addition to the agricultural exhibit is a hand-power combined cotton-gin, carding machine and spinning frame, which is an object of exceptional rarity.

The future of the Museum is bright. Plans have been outlined for material additions to the collections in all lines if time can be spared for field work. At the present time there is sufficient exhibit space to take care of a normal growth for several years.

There is a great deal of material on hand to be worked up into exhibit shape, which includes the Whale, Thresher Shark, large Alligator, Sailfish, and many other zoological and geological specimens. But the present inadequate force can only do so much and there is likely to be noticeable delay in the preparing and the final exhibition of some of the above-mentioned specimens.

INSTALLING NEW CASES

New modern cases for the exhibit of native gems and gemstones are nearing completion and this exhibit will be installed in a far more attractive manner than ever before. The geological collections in general are in course of being worked over for a more representative display.

The object always directly ahead of the Museum force is better service to the public. It has voluntarily adopted longer hours and the practice of keeping open on holidays and on the Saturday afternoons when most of the other State Departments take holiday.

The Museum is a valuable asset to the State and the expectation is to make it increasingly so. People sometimes ask, "when will the Museum be finished?" Such a condition should never come to pass. "A finished museum is a dead museum, and a dead museum is a useless museum!" No good museum was ever "finished," and it is not the idea that this institution will ever be allowed to suffer from dry-rot. There is always plenty of work ahead looking to its improvement and to increasing its value to the people of the State. There is no such condition as standing still. There must be movement—one way or the other—and the spirit of the State Museum of North Carolina knows no direction other than forward, and then forward again, to its continual and increasing betterment and towards the highest ideals of its work of adding to the knowledge and to the recreation of the public.

bove, A corner of the State Museum in Raleigh, showing exhibit cases and models of the *cean Sunfish*, *Mola mola*. *Below*, Many thousands of school children from all over North *arolina* visit the State Museum each year. (*Both, N. C. State Museum*)

The art of taxidermy. Mounting a deer. The rough body form with skull.

Above, Body covered with papier mâché, complete and ready for skin. *Below,* Completed mount of White-tailed Deer. (*All, N. C. State Museum*)

The Art of Taxidermy*

I<small>T</small> <small>WOULD HARDLY</small> seem necessary at this late date to have to explain that animals are no longer "stuffed." And yet it is necessary. Quite frequently is the question put to me, "What do you stuff 'em with?" and I have to explain again that "stuffing" specimens is about as extinct as is the use of the bow and arrow in hunting big game.

Taxidermy is an art. Not only is it necessary for the operator to know the natural attitudes of his subjects when alive but he must, in addition, possess the knowledge needed to properly model their skinned bodies in some kind of plastic material so that when the thinned down and prepared skin is fitted to the modelled body the result will show an animal with the proper

* Revised slightly from an article which appeared in the *Charlotte Daily Observer*, October 23, 1910. In reading this article the reader should bear in mind that although Brimley did not have the benefit of more recent techniques or the aid of "specialists" at this early date, he was able to turn out excellent work with the aid of readily available materials.

muscular development and, above all, "expression." Careful manipulation, skill in working out form and detail, and some knowledge of comparative anatomy—to say nothing of experience—are all necessary factors in achieving a good result.

Leaving out birds for the present as calling for less skill in mounting I shall proceed to take up the method of mounting mammals and explain the process in detail. Since the common Virginia deer is well known to everybody, quite enough so, at least, for most people to note at once whether or not a mounted specimen looks natural and life-like, a fine buck will be used for demonstration.

I have had skins sent in for mounting which were simply impossible. They might have made rugs or commercial pelts but, owing to the sender's lack of knowledge on the subject, had been ruined in the skinning so far as their ever being mounted was concerned. This brings us to the first principle, that is, the work of the taxidermist begins as soon as the animal is killed. The essential measurements must be made right then, or before the animal has been gutted, at least. The important measurements are as follows: length from tip of nose to base of tail; height at shoulder, with front legs arranged as when standing; distance from point where the thigh bone fits into the hip socket to where the upper bone of the fore leg articulates with the socket at lower end of the shoulder blade; girth, both back of the fore legs and forward of hind legs; girth of the neck in two places; length of neck, and other measurements if time and circumstances permit. The one measurement that I would rather have when only one is possible, is the distance between the articulating points of the hind and fore legs. All others may be approximated by an experienced operator. If you can, photograph the head from several different points of view, although I have often found that the camera is back at camp, or is out of order, or some other old thing will relieve you of this help in reproducing a good facial makeup.

Then comes the skinning. For a buck deer a straight incision must be made from the forward end of the brisket back to the root of the tail on the underside, and underneath the tail to the tip. Cross cuts are made on the inside of each pair of legs, running the cut to the back of each leg as the lower parts are reached. To get the skin over the horn and head the neck must be slit along the back, the cut running from the bone of each horn in a Y shape, the single line of the Y going far enough back for the opening to allow the skin being brought over the spreading horns easily. The skin should be removed carefully and cut just as little as possible since all cuts must be sewed up later and it may be difficult to hide the seams. The hoofs are left attached to the skin. Special care must be exercised on the head, the lips, eyelids, the regions around the horns and ears requiring extra care. The legs are then disjointed at the body and the leg and foot bones cleaned of flesh and saved. Likewise the skull must be cleaned and saved with the horns attached, and it is better to save the pelvis as well. The skin should be fairly well cleaned on the inside, the ears skinned out, the lips and nose split on the inside, and the whole skin thoroughly salted. Hang up the skin in the shade out of reach of dogs and, if the weather be warm, examine frequently, rubbing in more salt on any parts that seem to need it. When nearly dry the skin is ready to be made into a compact bundle and shipped to the workroom.

To get the skin into final shape for mounting, it should be treated to a tanning process in a lead-lined tank. One type of tanning solution consists of a mixture of certain proportions of common salt and sulphuric acid in water; it will do the trick in a day or two. Next comes the first part of the process that calls for any real skill. It consists in paring and thinning down the skin to the roots of the hair so that, in its final disposition, the skin may be fitted and adjusted to every contour of the model, with no danger of shrinkage in drying which will likely occur if skin is not thinned down. To accomplish the thinning process the hide is taken out of the tank drained, and thrown over a currier's beam. With certain knives made especially for this kind of work the inner layers of skin are shaved away. Two entirely different types of knives are used, one a double-edged curved blade with a handle at each end, and the other a heavy steel frame holding two steel blades with turned edges. The latter has one cross handle and the blades are held almost vertical to the skin. These tools must be kept as sharp as razors, and the blades held at the correct angles when in use, otherwise so many holes will be made in the hide that it will resemble a fragment of coarse seine rather than the covering of a self-respecting animal.

From the cartilages skinned from the ears artificial ones must be cut and hammered out of sheet lead or block tin, to replace the natural ones in the finished specimen. Then the hide goes back into the tank to await the completion of the manikin, the making of which will test the knowledge and artistic and mechanical skill of the operator to the fullest extent.

From the measurements of the animal taken in the flesh a board is cut about half an inch smaller all around than the longitudinal section of the middle of the deer's body, not including the neck. Previous to this, however, a sketch should be made as the mount is to appear when completed. Then, laying the body board on the floor, the leg bones are arranged in such positions as will give the desired attitude, with the articulating points properly adjusted on the board and the legs given the proper angles at the joints. This done, heavy wires are bent to conform to the bends in the limbs, when fitting close to them. Using these wires as models iron rods are cut and bent, sufficient length being left at the top of each for firmly fastening to the board, and also at bottom where the iron must go through the hoofs and the base of board on which the animal will eventually stand. The lower end of each rod must be perpendicular to the base, and must be threaded, with nuts cut to fit.

It may not sound like much of a job, this arranging leg bones, cutting, bending, and threading four rods, but it may take you a day or even two days of hard work if you are not content with anything less than perfection in the final attitude of the animal.

The leg irons are fastened to the body boards by wire or staples to insure a perfectly rigid attachment. The leg bones must be channeled out at certain places with cold chisels or saws to allow the irons to fit close and snug preventing their showing through the skin of the finished specimen. Now, the more or less wobbly frame is stood up on its feet and holes bored in a suitable base board to take the lower, threaded ends of the leg rods. A nut is run up on the rod to about the place where the hoof will hide it and the frame again stood up on its base. Some adjustment of nuts is almost certain to be necessary, and likewise some changes in the bending of the rods. This done to the satisfaction of the artist the leg bones are tightly fastened to the rods in several placed by wire or strong waxed thread. Nuts are now run on the threads of the rods projecting through the base board below, and set up tight. Now the whole frame will stand rigid and firm.

Into the base of the cleaned skull, previously cut out with a saw, a block of tough wood is securely fastened. Into this are fastened the ends of two neck rods, the other ends being fastened to the body board taking care to leave the neck of the proper length, as shown by the field measurements. Another rod is cut and fitted for the tail.

Next comes the rough shaping of the body, legs and neck which is done with medium mesh wire cloth, great care being taken not to make any part too large. Frequent reference must be made to the field measurements. A coat of shellac is next given the wire cloth to prevent rusting when the first coating of papier mâché is applied. The first stage of the mounting process may now be considered completed.

The second stage of the mounting process consists of building, on the wire frame, a complete reproduction of the skinned body of the animal as it would appear if it was possible to remove the skin with the animal standing in a natural attitude.

Papier mâché, which is a mixture of plaster of paris, good glue, paper pulp, and water, is now applied to the model. It is sticky stuff, but is easily worked, sets fairly quickly, and dries hard and smooth. The first coat is well worked into the meshes of the wire, some of it going through and keying on the inside. The first coat must be dampened again to allow the second coat to stick. Then the really artistic part of the performance begins. The round part of the body is not so difficult but the modelling of the muscles of the legs and neck calls for a good deal of knowledge and skill. The skin is removed from the tanning tank, drained of excessive moisture and occasionally tried on the model. By drawing it together underneath and noting the effects, the imperfections in form are brought out and changes in the model can be made accordingly. At last, after several days of this modelling and fitting, the operator reaches a point of more or less mental approval of his work, and the end of the second stage has been reached.

The skin is now laid out and thoroughly poisoned (white arsenic being commonly used) on the flesh side. The artificial ear cartilages are inserted and the hide is ready for its last and permanent fitting. Hot glue is painted over the entire surface of the model, the skin is carefully laid on and adjusted and the sewing up of the seams begins. Some taxidermists finish the head first, others leave it to the last. It is well to have two men working simultaneously on the sewing as it is a long and awkward job to neatly and securely sew up the four long seams. You cut out lunch and dinner these days, as it is necessary to hurry along while the skin is soft and moist. Wet cloths are kept on the parts not being worked, and your religion gets tested hard and often.

The treatment of the head is special. If the skinning of the eyes, lips, and nose was done correctly it will be found that the inner skin of these parts is still attached at the edges, so that sufficient papier mâché can be introduced between them and the outer skin to produce the natural fleshy appearance. The artificial eyes are set in and the eyelids modelled and fitted around them. The "tear pit," a depression below and in front of the eye must be tended to and the mouth, nose and ears worked out with fresh papier mâché, and all tacked and pinned into place. Care should be taken to give the swollen bases of the ears the full rounded appearance that these parts have in life.

All this being completed to the satisfaction of the operator, the specimen is set away to dry and finish such shrinkage as will always occur. This will take a month or two, varying with weather and facilities for artificial drying. The longer time for drying the better.

Last of all comes the cleaning and finishing. The whole animal is washed in lukewarm water and allowed to dry again. It is then lightly combed, brushed, and beaten to remove all salt, dirt and dust, and is then ready for painting of exposed parts. The nose is painted black with inside tinted as in life. The lips receive a touching up with the paint brush, as do the eyelids and the tear pit. The hoofs are cleaned,—and there stands your fine, handsome buck, a permanent reproduction of the noble animal as he stood in the swamplands.

"Do What You Can Now With What You Have"*

MOUNTING A WHALE SKELETON

THE TITLE OF THIS article was a favorite maxim of the late Doctor Frederick A. Lucas; and the wisdom of the advice contained therein becomes more and more apparent to me as time passes. An application of this maxim is indicated in the following description of the details of one major operation from which we have recently emerged with some credit to ourselves. And more particularly so for the reason that this operation consisted of the completion and installation of a really fine skeleton of a fifty-five foot sperm whale, starting with the partly decomposed body afloat in the Atlantic Ocean.

The scarcity of skeletons of this animal in museums, involving as it does the absence of experience in mounting skeletons of the species by most museum technicians, was another influencing factor. At the time our whale was secured there were but four

* *The Museum News,* VIII, No. 10 (November 15, 1930), 8-12.

adult sperm whale skeletons in museums in the continental United States.

We could find but little printed information that was of assistance in the work, and some that we did find proved erroneous; so individual initiative was frequently called into play. The "we" used throughout this paper refers to the writer and his associate in the North Carolina State Museum, Mr. Harry T. Davis.

A WHALE FOR THE TAKING

We were first offered the carcass as it lay almost in a man's front yard on Wrightsville Beach, a seaside resort near Wilmington, N. C., which offer we promptly declined, as the joker attached to the said offer included the removal of the body from the beach, an expensive operation.

The County Board of Health ordered the municipal authorities of the beach settlement to take it away from there and tow it 25 miles to sea, not later than high tide the following Sunday night. When Sunday came, conditions so far as we were concerned remained the same; so we cut off the projecting part of the lower jaw as a material record of the incident, and went home to weep over what we had lost. Unforeseen circumstances caused the loss of this jaw shortly after its acquisition, but it was later replaced by the jaw of another whale of approximately the same size.

Sunday night came and went, but nothing could be done in the face of the strong on-shore wind that blew in Sunday night and lasted about three days.

During these days a brilliant idea germinated and developed. Towing the body twenty-five miles to sea was modified to towing it twenty miles up the coast to Topsail Inlet, where a friend of ours owns about a mile of bare, uninhabited beach, the said friend granting us full permission to cut the carcass in on his property.

Thursday, on a moderating sea, two tugs made their first attempt near the top of flood tide, the finish of this day's work showing nothing but a parted hawser. With a new line, Friday's efforts were finally successful, the breaking of the body loose from its sandy bed being accomplished by both tugs—pulling tandem—backing in as close as the shoal water permitted, then steaming straight out to sea and taking up the slack of the line with a jerk. Once the carcass was in the water, the trip to Topsail Inlet was comparatively uneventful, though the tugs cast loose about a mile beyond the point indicated.

We had a small gas boat retained to go outside at the Inlet and pick up the whale when cast loose by the tugs. A phone call from Wilmington that the treasure was on its way resulted in a wire to our boatman, who promptly put out to sea.

But the wind had freshened, and when he reached the body he found that the towing people had left some heavy chains around the "small" of the tail, weighing the latter down so that he could find no part of the carcass to which to make fast his lines. The wind was on-shore, both whale and boat were drifting dangerously near the breakers, the boat was beginning to fill —when one of those justly-celebrated 110-foot rum chasers hove in sight.

The officer of the government boat, thinking our crew were at work dragging for a cache of liquor, shifted his helm and brought his boat tearing up, but on finding our men engaged in the perfectly legitimate operation of trying to salvage a very-much-spoiled sperm whale, he offered his assistance in towing the body inside the Inlet and making it fast to stakes driven in the sand of the beach.

That night, someone who needed some new Manila line, or who had a grudge against either us or our proposed operation, removed the lines holding the specimen in place, which thereby went adrift in the Sound, finally grounding on a shoal several hundred yards from the beach, from which position it was never again moved, except in pieces.

Mr. Davis handled the cutting-in, and two weeks of working a gang of Negro laborers on the exterior and interior of a putrid whale of large size must have strained his normally equable temperament to the limit. But he did the job, and he did it well!

OBJECTIONS MADE TO ODOR

It happened to be more convenient for us to secure our boat and cutting-in crew from a settlement several miles south of the Inlet. This action—perhaps backed by other influences—caused protests against the operation from people nearest to and north of the Inlet. Claims were made that the presence of the decaying carcass was causing loss to the fishermen and danger to the health of the community. One man wanted damages from the State at the rate of twenty dollars per day for alleged losses in the fish catch of his boat. Others wrote the County Board of Health, the State Board of Health, the Congressman from that district, and I believe that even the Governor of the State was approached.

But before starting operations we had taken the precaution to submit the matter to the chief official of the County Board of Health, from whom permission had been secured to carry on the work of dismemberment. We also knew, from having frequently used the place in fishing for channel bass, that the nearest residence to the scene of operations was nearly three miles distant, and as it turned out, the odor from our specimen was never more annoying than that from any one of the menhaden factories that dot certain sections of our coast-line, and around which people live and seem to thrive. But this phase of the matter called for various interviews with the Superintendent of the State Board of Health and quite a little correspondence, and caused us some worry—the threatening of lawsuits, etc.,—but all finally died down as we stuck to our guns.

MACERATION

Six and a half months of burial in a grave on the flat beach, just above high-water mark, and the bones were in condition to be moved nearer home. Mr. Davis took charge of the removal of the disarticulated skeleton from its sandy and salty grave to the mainland side of the sound, where it was to be loaded aboard a couple of three-ton trucks, while at Raleigh I made preparation for a re-burial.

The two truck-loads of bones reached Raleigh about dark on Saturday, November 9, 1928, and the trucks, which were the property of the State Highway Commission, were parked at the Truck Patch, the very large repair plant of the Commission, which adjoins the State Fair Grounds.

Inside the Fair Grounds, which are situated about four miles from the museum, a box was built on the surface of the ground, a site being selected on a gentle slope to secure the proper drainage. This measured 25 x 8 x 3½ feet, and 18 cubic yards of clean fresh-water sand were ordered and delivered close alongside it, the second burial taking place on November 12.

The earth floor of the box was first covered with a layer of sand about four inches deep, on which the tremendously heavy maxillaries were first put in place, the lifting of each of these bones requiring the services of six able-bodied laborers, the combined weight of the two bones being estimated at about two thousand pounds. Next came the cranium. This being large in all three dimensions, was set upright, its peak being about as high as the sides of the box. The arranging of the other bones was comparatively simple, but care was taken to keep the sand-shovellers busy and so to arrange the piece that each was completely imbedded in the sand, with no one bone touching any other. The completion of this burial-in-detail indicated that the bones alone occupied about four cubic yards of space.

Of course, a six and a half months burial in a beach grave, subject to salt-water treatment on each flood tide had by no means completed the necessary maceration. The whole outfit carried an odor approaching that of a fertilizer factory that had been turned into a home for unexpurgated skunks.

We found some slimy, partly-decomposed tissue still attached to a number of the pieces, particularly to the epiphyses of the larger vertebrae; and the combination of salt-water and sand and grease had formed a hard cement-like deposit on the surfaces of some of the bones. I neglected to state in the proper place that we improvised some wooden chisels and with them removed as much of the tissue and cement-like deposit as possible before placing these bones in the sand.

The smallest of the caudal vertebrae, the phalanges, and the other small bones and fragments, were tied up in tow sacks before being covered with sand. The sides of the box were tied across the top in several places to prevent their spreading as the sand settled, and the whole top was covered with wire netting of one-inch mesh.

During the ten months that followed, an occasional visit to the grave during the hot weather showed that the sand was properly retaining its moisture, and here I may mention another overlooked point, that the site had been selected with reference to proximity of a water supply and hose attachment, in case a wetting-down should be indicated during the maceration. During the summer, a thick growth of weeds, some of them six feet in height, made the grave a most conspicuous object.

The results of this ten months of treatment were, in the main, entirely satisfactory. A few of the bones still showed some grease-content, but nearly all of this was eliminated by a later treatment.

DRYING OUT THE BONES

We should in all likelihood have continued this maceration for a month or two longer had not the manager of the Fair Grounds indicated to us that he would need the ground cleared for the October Fair. The removal of the bones to the museum took place about the middle of September.

On reaching the museum, the maxillaries, together with five or six other large pieces of the skull, were placed on a wire-enclosed platform on the north side of our building, thus being exposed to the action of air and rain, but not to the sun. All of the others, comprising those that could be conveniently handled, were spread out on the flat roof of the central heating plant. This last lot was exposed to all the air, rain, and sunshine that came our way.

Approximately two months later, about the middle of November, a day arrived with freezing temperature indicated for the following night, and a hurried transfer was made of all the bones to the inside of the building. Then followed a thorough flushing with a garden hose, accompanied by an equally thorough scrubbing with stiff brushes, and such scraping with improvised wooden tools as seemed necessary.

Some of the pieces still showed a certain amount of grease-content, and these were treated with a weak lye solution and with household ammonia.

Wash day over, the bones were first drained—a great deal of the water-content running out readily—and everything was taken to the second floor of the museum and spread out to dry under the normal steamheat temperature of about 70 degrees. Some six weeks were allowed for drying.

PREPARATIONS FOR MOUNTING

A few days after Christmas, 1929, we started preparations for the actual mounting. The second-floor exhibition hall that had been selected for the installation of the skeleton has an open roof supported by a series of wooden trusses varying from twelve to fifteen feet apart, the lower members of which have a clearance of nineteen feet above the floor.

The first procedure, of course, was to have a competent engineer pass on the carrying capacity of these trusses, as applied to the additional loads we specified, with a view of providing reinforcements if necessary. The engineer's report being favorable, we next investigated the carrying capacity of I-beams of various dimensions. Allowing for more than a hundred per cent as a margin of safety, we selected a six-inch I-beam for the first two sections of the skeleton—the skull and the dorsal vertebrae with ribs, scapulars, and flippers attached—and a four-inch beam for the last two, one including the lumbar vertebrae and the other the caudal vertebrae. Supporting chains were next examined, a steel working chain of comparatively small size but with a greater factor of safety than in the case of the I-beams being chosen.

SUPPLIES

An open account was placed with a mill-supply house in town, to avoid the nuisance of having to make an official order for each item as needed or of bothering with invoices and statements before the completion of the job.

A handy-man carpenter was employed, together with an assistant, the former later on proving to be also a first-class blacksmith. We already possessed an anvil and we borrowed a forge, so that all the bending of iron straps and rods later on was carried out on the premises, also, a lot of welding, turning eyebolts, drilling holes in the straps, etc.

A selection of carriage bolts, running from ½-inch by 2 inches up to ⅝ by 20 inches, was ordered and delivered. Also some 18-inch car bits in various diameters up to 1 inch were selected, and others ordered lengthened to 30 inches over all. As I remember now, the longest hole we had to bore through solid bone was 28 inches. Carriage bolts were selected on account of their low, round heads, so much less conspicuous than the heavy, square head of the machine bolt, and also for the reason that the square shank just below the head prevents the turning of the bolt when a tight-fitting nut is encountered.

We already posessed a two-ton chain hoist and several sets of block and tackle; so we were now about set for the actual mounting of the skeleton.

PUTTING THE SKELETON TOGETHER

The cranium itself, which we estimated to weigh some five or six hundred pounds, was now set up and blocked in position on a low-platform truck fitted with rubber-tired castors, the truck being held in position by strips of wood nailed to the floor.

The remainder of the skull was in many pieces, some the result of breakage in the many handlings and some of a natural separation of the individual bones at their sutures. It was now found that the factors of warpage and shrinkage had to be faced. One at a time, places for the various bones and pieces were found, each item, particularly the heavy ones, requiring a good deal of time and some mental anguish in the placing, temporary blocking in place being in order as the fit was gradually adjusted. When an item reached its final adjustment, the diameter and approximate length of the required bolts or lag screws was determined, the places and directions of the holes marked, and the holes bored.

And here is a random note for the uninitiated in whale skeletons: Writers on the skeletal framework of whales are quite fond of describing the softness and spongy texture of the bones, but I do not call to mind a single writer who has anything to say about the hardness of the outer shell of many of them. There was a lot of heavy sweating in bearing down on the braces holding the cutting bits in the case of many of the holes we had to bore, and some of the bits were bent out of shape in the effort. But nearly all of the holes in our skeletons were finally cut with ordinary commercial car bits, though in some cases, the hole had to be started with a chisel.

Warpage and shrinkage have already been mentioned, and now we were in the thick of it, the first instances we encountered being in the broad, thin plates that constitute the high crest of the cranium. We would fit and then bolt up a section, turning the nuts up fairly tight and, at intervals of a day or two, take up the nuts until the individual bones finally assumed an approximately correct relationship with one another. In some cases, where bolts proved unsuitable, large wood screws, or lag screws, were substituted. But heavy bolts were invariably used where any considerable strain was expected to develop.

The placement of the two massive maxillaries proved, perhaps, the major problem of the whole operation. One of them was loaded on a second low-platform truck and rolled into its approximate position. Then, the truck was locked in place and the bone levered and blocked to a rough fit. This called for a turning on its long axis in addition to movements in both vertical and horizontal planes. Maxillary No. 2 called for a different treatment as lateral movement was only possible in one direction, movement in the other being blocked by the companion bone already in place. A three-quarter inch hole was bored through the flat of the bone as nearly as we could guess at its center of gravity. The head end of a five-eighths by twenty-four inch machine bolt

A Sperm Whale washed up on Wrightsville Beach. The skeleton of this specimen is shown in subsequent pictures as it was mounted in the State Museum. (*N. C. State Museum*)

Skeleton of the Sperm Whale in place in the Museum. (*N. C. State Museum*)

The skeleton in the process of being assembled. (*N. C. State Museum*)

The completed skeleton of the Sperm Whale. (*N. C. State Museum*)

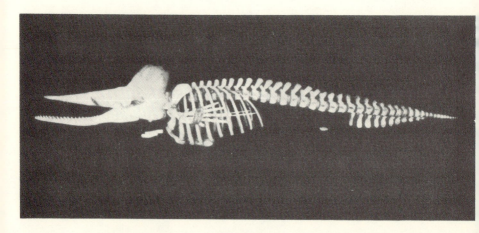

was heated and turned into a short-turn hook. The threaded end was passed through the hole from above and the nut put on over a broad washer.

A substantial overhead support being provided, our chain hoist came into play, and with but little effort the bone was brought to its approximate position. But "approximate" is right! It was easy enough to see exactly where the basal end of the bone fitted, but to get it there was something entirely different. Twist it slightly to the right and it caught in one place; turn it a fraction to the left and the other edge failed to make the grade, and similar conditions developed in the final fitting of its companion bone.

Space is lacking in this paper to go into full details of how we secured the permanent adjustments. In fact, it is doubtful if such would be of any value, as no exactly similar problems would ever again occur, but the results were secured in some instances by readjustments of some of the adjoining bones. One of these was the running of a seven-eighths inch rod nearly seven feet long and threaded for six inches at each end through the lower forward part of the big semi-circular crest and slowly drawing the sides a little closer together at the rate of a fraction of an inch a day.

Some of the longest holes and the hardest boring were incident to locking the maxillaries in place, and the fitting of these two bones covered a period of about four days. Iron straps were used in making the tie, these being installed wherever possible inside the hollow of the skull, and therefore largely out of sight in the finished specimen. Most of these straps were ¼-inch by 2 inches, though the band that almost encircles the pair of maxillaries is three-eighths by two inches. This last band, both on account of the short turns and of the increased thickness, had to be bent hot, but cold bending was used wherever practicable. The curves for the three-eighths inch band were made from a pattern of heavy, stiff wire, easily slipped off over the tapering forward ends of the bones. Of course, the band as first shaped required a lot of minor changes in the actual fitting, but a good job resulted. The emplacement of this was made to coincide as closely as possible to the center of gravity of the maxillaries, for the support of which it was mainly provided.

A lot of difficulty was encountered in making the ends of this strap, which lapped over the outer edges of the bones and continued almost to their upper inside edges, fall directly over the lines of the under portion of the iron. But an adjustment was finally reached so that the five-eighths inch eyebolts that were to engage with two of the supporting chains were each finally run through a hole in the upper member of the strap, through the bone itself, and through the strap's lower member, and the nut on the lower end of the bolt turned down hard. A final element of safety was to cut off the end of the bolt about an eighth of an inch beyond the nut and to expand the end.

A temporary support was placed under the maxillaries near their distal ends. Then the whole of their weight was transferred to the low-platform truck number 2, and they were blocked and wedged into their final position. The two trucks were now tied together with planks nailed to both, leaving the whole skull, minus the lower jaw, on one free-moving body when the fastenings of the trucks to the floor had been removed. Two more eyebolts were now set in the cranium and the skull rolled beneath its position for hanging. With tackles and chain hoist, the skull was raised sufficiently for the attachment of the lower jaw.

Mention was made earlier in this paper of the loss of the lower jaw of our whale, but we were lucky in finding a liberal-minded owner of a jaw from a whale of approximately the same size as ours, which we acquired. The sample teeth that came with the substitute showed wear from age, while the original teeth in our specimen were immaculate, showing no sign of wear whatever; so the former were useless as models. Fortunately, the originals we had to reproduce had been carefully examined and measured by us, so but little difficulty was encountered in making patterns from which to model the set we needed. Forty-two in all were made—and our skeleton has been complimented on the perfection of its teeth.

After some experimenting, the following was the method followed in making our set. First, of course, came the making of the patterns, and then the moulds therefrom.

A quantity of dental plaster was mixed dry with the small proportion of yellow ochre indicated by the experiments. The models, as they came from the moulds, reinforced with burlap and made hollow at the root, were dried near a radiator. When dry, they were pointed up and given a soaking in boiled linseed oil. This was followed by wiping off the unabsorbed oil and drying a second time. The next treatment consisted of a liberal coating of a thin paste of turpentine and beeswax. This was allowed to stay on about twenty-four hours. The surplus wax was then wiped off and the tooth given a good rubbing with canton flannel. The resulting product is hard, fairly tough, and carries just about the color and the degree of polish desired. The teeth were set in the grooves with ordinary prepared papier mâché.

The only description of the sternum of a sperm whale that we could find states that it is composed of three bones, while ours had five. Among the few bones that had to be replaced outright were two of the smaller caudal vertebrae and two small chevrons; that is, outside of some of the phalanges, which seldom seem to be delivered in full. Two hyoids and a double pelvic bone are present, and we have the eleventh pair of ribs, which are rudimentary in character.

The skull completed and hung, with the atlas bolted in place —the other six cervicals being fused—the remainder of the job was comparatively simple, though calling for time and a lot of hard work.

The dorsal and lumbar sections each have two seven-eighths inch rods running through the centra of the vertebrae; the caudal section, only one. Each of the sections is dowelled and tied to its neighbor.

Before the holes through the vertebrae centra were bored for the rods, a formula for the spacing of the vertebrae was worked out and blocks of white pine of the various degrees of thickness required were cut to fill in the spaces originally occupied by the cushions of fibrous tissue that provide for the side sweeps of the hinder part of the body and tail of the animal—in both vertical and horizontal planes—used in its daily evolutions. These blocks were nailed one to each centrum, as provided. The two holes were then drilled through each centrum and its attached block. When a section of vertebrae had been bolted and wedged up to its required curve, a strip of galvanized wire cloth of ½-inch mesh was tacked around each block separating two vertebrae, and a smooth finish to the joint worked out with papier mâché. The dorsal section was then hoisted for the attachment of the ribs, scapulae, sternum, and flippers, at such a height that the longest rib just cleared the floor. The final attachment of the supporting chains to the I-beams in giving each section its proper angle or curve, the joining up of the sections, the hanging of the chevrons and the hyoids, and the finishing touches called for here and there, were mainly questions of elementary mechanics, with of course, some little knowledge of a whale's anatomy.

REPAIR WORK

A lot of small repair work had to be carried out as we progressed, but I do not call to mind that any noticeable departure from well-known methods was called into play. We used a good deal of the afore-mentioned quarter-inch galvanized wire cloth in carrying out some of the repairs; and, to lessen the quantity of papier mâché naturally forced through the large meshes, some rather coarsely chopped tow was mixed with the dry mâché before the water was added. This addition of tow also increased the toughness and binding quality of the mâché, and tended to show a rougher dry surface.

A thin coat of kalsomine, tinted to simulate the color of dry bone as nearly as possible, was given the whole skeleton; the exposed bolt heads and iron straps, together with the supporting chains, were painted with aluminum bronze—and the job was finished.

PHOTOGRAPHING

The room in which the skeleton hangs is forty feet wide, so it was of course impossible to secure a right-angle full length picture at one exposure. We have one picture taken almost head-on, which is nearly all head! The composite picture was made from the pick of some nine or ten negatives taken from various points at varying angles, and I think it is nearly as good as could be obtained.

We were particularly anxious to get a good photograph of this skeleton for the reason that we were so much hampered in our work by not being able to secure anything of the kind for guidance, and it is our hope that our pictures may prove of assistance to other museum workers in the future.

The actual mounting of the skeleton covered a period of about six weeks, about half of which was devoted to the skull, and perhaps the main point to be emphasized is the fact that we did not call for the assistance of specialists—such being beyond our financial reach, for one thing—in the mounting of our sperm whale skeleton, but *we did what we could, THEN, with what we had!*

Index

INDEX